Funny Money

A comedy

Ray Cooney

Samuel French — London
New York - Toronto - Hollywood

FOR AMATEUR PRODUCTION ENQUIRIES

UNITED KINGDOM AND WORLD EXCLUDING NORTH AMERICA

plays@SamuelFrench-London.co.uk

020 7255 4302/01

Each title is subject to availability from Samuel French,

depending upon country of performance.

FUNNY MONEY

First performed at the Theatre Royal, Windsor, on 4th May 1994, with the following cast:

Jean Perkins	Carol Hawkins
Henry Perkins	Ray Cooney
Bill	Hugh Lloyd
Davenport	Alfred Marks
Slater	Trevor Bannister
Betty Johnson	Anita Graham
Vic Johnson	Henry McGee
Passer-by	Ron Aldridge

Directed by Ray Cooney
Décor by Douglas Heap

Subsequently produced at the Playhouse Theatre, London, on 2nd October 1995, with the following cast:

Jean Perkins	Sylvia Syms
Henry Perkins	Ray Cooney
Bill	Charlie Drake
Davenport	Peter Ellis
Slater	Trevor Bannister
Betty Johnson	Lynda Baron
Vic Johnson	Henry McGee
Passer-by	Ron Aldridge

Directed by Ray Cooney
Décor by Douglas Heap

CHARACTERS

Jean Perkins, a pretty but ordinary woman in her late 40s

Henry Perkins, an insignificant man in his early 50s

Bill, a middle-aged London taxi driver of spirit

Davenport, a sparse middle-aged man with a knowing glint in his eye

Slater, a solicitous and kindly soul—until provoked

Betty Johnson, a buxom and cheerful woman in her late 40s

Vic Johnson, a brash man with feet of clay

Passer-by, a large man

The action of the play—which is continuous—takes place in the Fulham house of Henry and Jean Perkins

Time — a winter evening

*Other plays by Ray Cooney
published by Samuel French Ltd:*

It Runs in the Family
Out of Order
Run for Your Wife!
Two Into One
Why Not Stay for Breakfast?
(written with Gene Stone)
Wife Begins at Forty
(written with Arne Sultan and Earl Barret)

ACT I

The living-room of Henry and Jean Perkins in Fulham, which reflects a middle-class background. Through the windows and front door (when it's open) can be seen a front garden, and the house is clearly set on a corner

The front door, DL, leads directly into a porch area. There is a door to the kitchen in the centre of the right wall and a door to the dining-room above the front door. In the dining-room can be seen a laid-up dining table for four people. Stairs UC lead up and off R to the bedrooms. There is a cupboard in the rear wall to the left of the stairs. In the UR corner of the room is a sideboard on which is a selection of liquor bottles and glasses, the Yellow Pages *and a vase of flowers*

The room is quite tidy but "lived in" and the furniture is "comfortable" rather than new. There is a long settee DRC and an armchair DLC. Below the kitchen door is a table on which is a radio. There is a small desk DL and above this is a cuckoo clock. In front of the settee is a coffee table and to the left of the settee is a small table on which is the telephone

It is a winter evening and the Lights are on. The stage is empty. The radio is playing the William Tell *overture*

After a moment, Jean comes out of the kitchen. She is wearing a pretty dress covered by an apron and is carrying a candle in a silver holder. She hurries through into the dining-room. After a brief moment, she returns from the dining-room without the candle. She looks at her watch and then hurries to the front door. She looks left and right and then closes the front door. She then hurries into the kitchen. After a moment, she returns from the kitchen carrying a bowl and a wooden spoon. She hurries to the front door, opens it, looks left and right and closes it again. She looks at her watch

Jean (*to herself*) You wretched man, Henry.

Jean then exits into the kitchen. After a moment, she returns from the kitchen with a bowl of peanuts and a bottle of sparkling rosé. She puts the peanuts on the table DR and switches the radio off. She marches into the dining-room with the bottle of wine. She places the bottle of wine on the dining-room table, enters and exits into the kitchen

The front door opens and Henry Perkins appears. He is wearing a suit and raincoat and carrying a briefcase. He is breathing heavily and looks dazed. He stands in the doorway

Jean enters from the kitchen, carrying a tray on which are four plates and four sets of cutlery. Without seeing Henry, who is masked by the open front door, she marches into the dining-room

Henry, still in a daze, closes the door behind him, walks to the settee and sits, putting his briefcase on the floor

Jean enters from the dining-room and opens the front door. She looks left and right, then looks at her watch

(*To herself*) You wretched man, Henry!

Henry is still in a daze and doesn't react. Jean bangs the door shut and starts to move towards the kitchen. She sees Henry

(*Startled*) Ah!

Henry looks at her blankly

Oh, Henry! You gave me a…! Where have you been, for heaven's sake?

Henry looks away blankly

You're nearly an hour late! Vic and Betty will be here in a minute.

Henry looks at her blankly

For your birthday dinner!

Henry looks away

Why on earth didn't you phone if you were working late in the office?
Was the train delayed?

Henry looks at her

Say something, Henry!

Henry looks away

Henry (*suddenly*) *Yellow Pages!*
Jean What?
Henry *Yellow Pages!* (*He hurries to the sideboard and gets out the*
Yellow Pages *directory*)
Jean What do you want *Yellow Pages* for?
Henry (*searching*) Travel Agents! No! They'll be closed. British Air-
ways! (*He hurriedly flips through the pages*)
Jean Have you been in some sort of accident?
Henry (*reading*) Airlines—American Airlines. British Airways! 0181
897 4000. (*He throws the directory over his shoulder and sits on the
settee. He then places the telephone on the coffee table in front of him*)
Jean What do you want British Airways for?
Henry (*dialling*) 0181 897 4000.
Jean Henry! Vic and Betty are coming——

Henry finishes dialling

—for dinner!
Henry (*into the phone*) British Airways?
Jean It's your birthday!
Henry (*into the phone*) I'd like to book two air flights please.
Jean Air flights?
Henry (*into the phone*) For tonight.
Jean What?!
Henry (*into the phone*) Anywhere.
Jean Henry!
Henry (*into the phone*) Yes, you heard me, anywhere. Well, anywhere
you don't need a special visa for. Holland, Sweden, France, Germany,
Denmark, Spain.
Jean What's the matter with you, we've got Vic and Betty at six
thirty——

Henry (*into the phone*) What? ... Time of flight? Hang on a second. (*To Jean*) How long will it take to get to London Airport?
Jean You've been drinking!
Henry By taxi.
Jean I can smell it on your breath. Whisky! You've been drinking.
Henry It's six thirty now.
Jean Put that phone down!
Henry Taxi, at seven, Heathrow, eight. Check in. (*Into the phone*) Nine o'clock!
Jean I shall stay calm, Henry.
Henry (*into the phone*) Yes, any flight around nine o'clock.
Jean I'm going to start getting angry very soon.
Henry Go and pack. And get the passports. (*He indicates the desk* L)
Jean Henry...
Henry Only one suitcase! A small one. (*Into the phone*) And we want to go First Class.
Jean You'll make me cry, Henry.
Henry (*to Jean*) Just a change of underclothes. We'll buy everything else when we get there.
Jean Get where?
Henry (*into the phone*) Barcelona? Great! ... Twenty-one fifteen hours. What's that in real time? ... Nine fifteen p.m., excellent!
Jean (*starting to cry*) Henry, please...!
Henry (*into the phone*) I don't care, smoking, non-smoking. Can I pay in cash at the airport?
Jean (*crying*) It's your birthday. (*She sits in the armchair and buries her head in her hands*)
Henry (*into the phone*) Terrific. Two First Class, Barcelona. What? Oh no, singles. Yes, singles, we're not coming back.

Jean starts to cry loudly

(*Into the phone*) Mr and Mrs Henry Perkins. ... Yes pick up the tickets half an hour before check- in, will do. Thanks for your assistance. Bye. (*He replaces the receiver*)
Jean Henry——
Henry Ssh, ssh, ssh. (*He lifts the receiver again and dials*)
Jean Who are you phoning now?
Henry Toothbrush, toothpaste and razor, that's all I need. (*Into the phone*)

Hello, Fulham Taxis? I need a car to take two of us to London Airport immediately. ... Fifteen minutes, brilliant! Make it ten if you can. ... Mr Perkins, 42 Elgar Avenue. ... That's right, it's on the corner. (*He replaces the receiver*)
Jean Henry——
Henry Jean, listen!

Henry rises, but Jean sits him on the settee and sits beside him

Jean No, you listen! You've been drinking and it's affected your brain. You're not used to alcohol and you've gone funny.
Henry No, I haven't gone funny.
Jean Yes, you have! I don't know what's happened to you exactly, but we are not travelling to Barcelona tonight. We have Vic and Betty coming round for your birthday dinner.

During the ensuing speech, Henry picks up his briefcase. He puts it on the coffee table and opens it to show Jean the contents

They've been working you far too hard at the office. It's probably not serious, just one of those temporary breakdowns. I don't think it's a blood clot. (*She stops on realizing what's in the briefcase. It is packed with bundles of fifty pound notes*) What's that?
Henry Seven hundred and thirty-five thousand pounds.
Jean (*blankly*) What is it?
Henry Cash.
Jean (*blankly*) But what is it?
Henry Money. Cash. Seven hundred and thirty-five thousand pounds. All in fifties. Fourteen thousand, seven hundred of them. Fourteen thousand, seven hundred fifty pound notes. Seven hundred and thirty-five thousand pounds in used notes.
Jean (*sternly*) What is it, Henry?
Henry It's a bloody fortune, Jean. Passports! (*He goes to get the passports from the desk* L)

She starts to lift up the bundles which are wrapped in elastic bands. The notes are clearly used

Jean Henry, how did all this money get into your briefcase?

Henry That's just it. It's not my briefcase.

Jean What are you talking about?

Henry I got off the Underground train at Fulham Broadway—like I always do—with my briefcase and I started to walk home, you know, the way I always do, down Aylmer Road. Have you moved our passports?

Jean Bottom drawer. Get on with it.

Henry Well, it was a bit nippy, so I thought I'd put my gloves and scarf on. Now, they were in my briefcase—so I stopped and flipped open my briefcase. Only, it wasn't my briefcase.

Jean Not your briefcase?

Henry Ah, passports! (*He shoves them in his pocket*)

Jean What do you mean, "not your briefcase"?

Henry I must have left my briefcase on the train and taken this one by mistake. Or else somebody took mine and left theirs. (*He crosses delightedly to the briefcase*)

Jean Why didn't you take it back right away?

Henry I was in shock. How would you feel if you opened your handbag to powder your nose and found seven hundred and thirty-five thousand pounds in there?

Jean How do you know the exact amount?

Henry I counted it.

Jean Counted it? In the middle of Aylmer Road?

Henry No, in *The Prince of Wales* pub.

Jean I thought you'd been drinking.

He sits Jean on the settee, sits beside her and surveys the cash

Henry I had to pull myself together. I had to think what to do.

Jean Taken it to the London Transport Lost Property Office, that's what you should have done.

Henry So I ordered a large whisky and then went into the Gents loo.

Jean The loo?

Henry To check if I hadn't been seeing things. I hadn't. I sat on the lavatory seat and counted it all out.

Jean Henry!

Henry Then I went back to the bar and had that double whisky.

Jean Then what?

Henry I had another one. Then I went back to the Gents, sat on the loo and counted it all over again.

Jean No wonder you're an hour late.

Henry Actually, I had one more whisky and another sit on the loo before I'd finished. I just couldn't believe it.

Jean Henry!

Henry Jean! We'll never get another chance like this as long as we live. We've got to grab it with both hands.

Jean We can't just up and leave at a moment's notice.

Henry Oh, yes we can. Oh! We're travelling First Class, I'll keep some of these for tips on the flight. (*He puts a few notes in his pocket*)

Jean It's not our money, Henry.

Henry It is now. Go and pack.

Jean Henry, it's stealing!

Henry Oh, no! I gave that a lot of thought when I was sitting on *The Prince of Wales* loo. It seems to me this money is ill-gotten gains. I mean, it must be, right? Used notes all bundled up in elastic bands. It'll be payment to a Mr Nasty for some illicit transaction. This is cash that doesn't show in anyone's books—it won't be reflected in anyone's accounts—no income tax or VAT will have been paid on it. This money doesn't exist—so if it doesn't exist, I can't have stolen it!

Jean Henry——

Henry Jean, my conscience is clear. I've worked very hard for nothing for thirty years and at long last I've received my bonus.

Jean But the police will——

Henry (*interrupting*) The police will never get involved because the loss of this cash will never be reported to the police. Now go and pack that suitcase.

Jean Henry——

Henry Go and pack. And just a sponge bag and a couple of pairs of underpants for me.

Jean Henry, I want to have dinner with Vic and Betty. I want to have our roast chicken! I want to stay here at number 42 Elgar Avenue!

Henry Jean, you don't understand. We can't stay here. I can't go back to the office. I've burned my bridges.

Jean But it's not too late.

Henry Yes, it is! If I've got Mr Nasty's briefcase, he's got mine. It's got my office stuff in it. Tomorrow morning, Mr Nasty will call at the office looking for his briefcase and me. By that time we've got to be a thousand miles away booked into some Spanish hotel as Mr and Mrs Shufflebottom.

Jean Henry, he'll come looking for us. It won't matter if we're Shufflebottom, Ramsbottom or Sidebottom, he'll come looking for us.

Henry He won't know where to find us.

Jean He'll report us to the police. *They'll* find us. Interpol. It'll be awful.

Henry It'll be lovely! Because there won't be any Interpol. Because Mr Nasty can't go to the police. I told you. Mr Nasty has fiddled seven hundred and thirty-five thousand pounds. And now the fiddler has been well and truly fiddled! Ha, ha! By yours truly. Henry A. Perkins!

Jean is amazed

Jean I've never seen you like this, Henry.

Henry I've never bloody felt like this, that's why.

Jean I liked you as you were—a bit of a wimp.

Henry Well those days are over! (*He starts to sing "We're both going to sunny Spain" while closing the briefcase*)

Jean Henry, I don't want to go to Barcelona.

Henry Don't be daft. You love it in Spain. We've had three holidays there.

Jean Holidays, yes! We weren't emigrating.

Henry All right, if you don't like Barcelona, we'll just stay overnight, then fly on somewhere else—Australia, Bermuda, Bali... (*He holds up the briefcase*) We'll buy Bali!

Jean I like it here, Henry. I don't want to move. What about the family?

Henry What family? We haven't got any family.

Jean Alf and Doris.

Henry Doris is your second cousin and you haven't seen her for twenty years.

Jean I send her a Christmas card.

Henry Send her one from Barcelona. Now go and pack that suitcase.

The doorbell rings

Jean Oh, God!

Henry That'll be Vic and Betty. I'll pack the suitcase—you get rid of them. (*He moves to the stairs*)

Jean What'll I say to them? They've come to dinner.

Henry Tell them to go to the Savoy and have dinner on me!

He takes some fifty pound notes from his pocket, throws them to Jean and exits upstairs still carrying the briefcase

Jean (*calling upstairs, almost crying*) But it's your birthday! (*She picks up the fifty pound notes. To herself*) It's his *birthday*.

The doorbell rings. Jean goes to the front door

(*Opening the door*) I'm sorry I took so long——

She stops on seeing a man standing there in a raincoat. He is Detective Sergeant Davenport

Oh. I thought you were—er—I was expecting someone else. (*She hastily stuffs the money in her dress*)
Davenport Detective Sergeant Davenport, madam. Fulham CID.
Jean (*trying to be nonchalant*) Fulham CID.
Davenport That's right, madam. (*He flashes his pass and walks in*) I was wondering if I could have a word with the gentleman of the house.
Jean The gentleman?
Davenport That would be your husband, would it, madam?

She closes the door and hurries to him

Jean What exactly—er—could you tell me what the problem is?
Davenport I'd rather see your husband, Mrs—er ——?
Jean Perkins.
Davenport Ah, Perkins.
Jean He's upstairs at the moment.

There is a slight pause

Would you like a peanut?
Davenport No, thank you.

The doorbell rings

Jean (*jumping*) Ohh! (*To Davenport*) Sorry. I'm a bit—er... (*Calling*) Henry! (*Then to Davenport*) That's my husband—"Henry".

Davenport smiles and nods

Excuse me, Sergeant, I'll just see who—er——
Davenport Of course.
Jean I expect it will be Vic and Betty. They're having dinner with us tonight. (*She smiles awkwardly at Davenport*)

He nods and smiles politely back

The Johnsons. Vic and Betty. Do sit down.

He goes to sit

(*Yelling upstairs*) Henry!!!

Davenport, in the middle of sitting, reacts. Jean smiles at him. He sits

Yes. Dinner at home. Just the four of us. Henry and me. Betty and Vic.
It's his birthday.
Davenport That's nice.
Jean Henry's, not Vic's.
Davenport Ah.
Jean I don't know when Vic's is.
Davenport You'd better let them in.
Jean Yes. Henry won't be a... He's—er—getting dressed. In his birthday
suit. Oh! I don't mean he has no—er——
Davenport No.
Jean I'll—er... (*She opens the door*)

Bill steps in

Bill Here we are!
Jean Oh, I thought——
Bill You thought fifteen minutes, and I made it in ten.
Jean I beg your pardon?
Bill Fulham Taxis.
Jean (*nervously*) Oh! Yes.
Bill I'm Bill. Well now, London Airport. How many cases?
Jean (*trying to make light of it*) Cases?
Bill To go.
Jean Oh! Cases! For the—er—airport. Somebody flying off! (*She smiles
at Davenport*)

Davenport just looks blank

(*To Davenport*) Yes, it's not—er—my—er... (*She vaguely waves her hand upstairs. She looks at Davenport and smiles. To Davenport*) It's my—er—sister. She's staying with us. She has been. She's leaving this evening. London Airport.

Bill No, it's Mr Perkins.

Jean What?

Bill The docket says "Mr Perkins". (*He shows a slip of paper*)

Jean No. Mr Perkins isn't going anywhere. It's his birthday. No, Mr Perkins just made the booking.

Bill Oh.

Jean No, it's my sister who's leaving—flying off. (*She smiles at Davenport*)

He smiles back

Bill So, how many cases?

Jean I'm not sure—er—"Bill" did you say it was?

Bill Yes, "Bill".

Jean Yes. Why don't you wait in the taxi, Bill? Mr Perkins will help with the cases. My—er—sister's not quite ready yet.

Bill Fine. I'm parked just round the corner. Where's she flying off to?

Jean I beg your pardon?

Bill Your sister. What's her destination?

Jean hesitates, smiles at Davenport

Jean (*turning to Bill*) Australia.

Bill Australia! Down under, eh?

Jean Yes, she emigrated. She's been here for a visit. (*She smiles at Davenport*) Now she's going back. To Sydney.

Bill Very nice. OK, I'm in that side street. Just give me a shout when the pair of them are ready.

Jean The pair of them?

Bill The docket says two people. That's a pair, madam. (*He shows her*)

Jean Yes, that's right. My sister and her husband. That's why she emigrated. He's Australian. (*She smiles at Davenport*)

Davenport smiles and nods

(*To Bill*) I'll tell them you're parked around the corner.

Bill That's right. (*To Davenport*) Nice to have met you.

Bill exits

Jean smiles at Davenport

Jean Hectic here tonight.
Davenport Certainly seems that way. Do you have something in the oven?
Jean (*confused*) I beg your pardon?
Davenport Dinner with your friends. The Johnsons.
Jean Oh, yes.
Davenport And you seem a bit distracted.
Jean No, that's all in hand. Roast chicken.
Davenport Pity your sister and her husband are going to miss it.
Jean What? Oh, yes! Er—Adelaide. Adelaide and—er—Percy. No, they've got to catch their aeroplane.
Davenport (*chuckling*) Still, Sydney! By the time they've finished that journey, they'll have had half a dozen dinners.
Jean (*trying to laugh*) Yes!

Henry hurries downstairs, carrying his raincoat with the briefcase and a small suitcase. Without seeing Davenport, he places the briefcase and the raincoat on the chair

Henry Right, all packed!
Jean Henry!
Henry Did you deal with Vic and Betty?
Jean Henry! We have a visitor. (*She indicates Davenport*)

Davenport stands up. Henry turns

Henry A vis—— Oh. Ah! Fulham Taxis, brilliant!
Davenport Fulham police, actually.
Henry Great! (*He goes to hand the suitcase to Davenport, but stops*) Fulham police?
Davenport Detective Sergeant Davenport. CID. (*He flashes his card*)
Henry (*cheerfully*) Yes, that's fine. (*He nonchalantly covers the briefcase with his raincoat*) What's the problem, Sergeant? Neighbours been complaining about something?

Davenport You're Mr Perkins, are you, sir? Mr Henry Perkins?
Henry The very same.
Davenport I wonder if I could have a word with you, sir.
Henry (*expansively*) Certainly. What about?
Davenport If Mrs Perkins wouldn't mind, I'd prefer to see you alone.
Henry Alone? Of course!
Davenport Although I don't mind waiting until your wife's sister has gone.
Henry (*blankly*) My wife's er...?
Jean (*weakly*) He's referring to Adelaide.
Henry (*blankly*) Adelaide?
Davenport They're just about to leave, I gather.
Henry (*to Jean*) When he says "they"...
Jean Adelaide and—Percy.

Henry can only manage a smile at Davenport

Davenport Back down under.

Henry looks down at the floor

Henry Back?
Jean Down under. Sydney.
Henry Adelaide, Percy and Sidney?
Jean Thanks for bringing their luggage down.
Henry Oh, pleasure!
Jean I really don't think the Sergeant need wait for Percy and Adelaide to leave, do you, Henry?
Henry Definitely not. Nor Sidney. Police business first. Shall we go into the kitchen, Sergeant?

The doorbell rings

Jean Oh, my God!
Henry That'll be the taxi. Tell it to wait.
Jean Bill's already here.
Henry Who's Bill?
Jean Fulham Taxis.
Henry Ah, great!

Jean For Adelaide and Percy.

Henry Ah, yes!

Jean It'll be Vic and Betty Johnson!

Henry Just get rid of them.

Jean But we've invited them to your birthday dinner.

Henry Well, tell them to leave their presents and go! (*To Davenport*) I've
decided to have the wife all to myself tonight. It's my birthday, isn't it,
not Vic's. (*To Jean*) They'll understand. Tell them we're going to bed.
(*To Davenport*) After I've satisfied the Sergeant, of course. (*Realizing*)
Oh! When I say satisfied... I mean, after I've answered the Sergeant's
questions. (*He opens the kitchen door*) After you, Sergeant.

Jean Henry, I can't cope!

Henry Of course you can!

Jean No, I can't.

Henry You can. (*To Davenport*) She can. She just thinks she can't.

The doorbell rings—Jean jumps

Jean Aaah!

Davenport Perhaps it would be better, sir, if *you* answered the door and
I'll wait for you in the kitchen.

Jean That's a good idea.

Henry (*at a loss*) Yes, all right. Shouldn't take a moment.

Davenport No. And by the time you've seen your friends off, your in-
laws might have gone, too.

Henry What in-laws? Oh! The in-laws—Adelaide and—er—Percy. Yes,
they're upstairs, packed and ready to go. (*He chuckles at Davenport and
indicates for him to go into the kitchen*)

Davenport Make it as snappy as you can, Mr Perkins. I do have a line of
enquiry to follow.

Henry Of course! Put the kettle on for a cuppa, will you?

Davenport looks at Henry levelly and exits into the kitchen

Jean Henry! You said the man wouldn't go!

Henry What man wouldn't go where?

Jean The man who's got your briefcase. You said he wouldn't contact the
police.

Henry (*indicating the kitchen*) He might not have called about the
briefcase! (*He picks up the briefcase*)

Jean Of course it's about the briefcase. Why do you think he wants to see you alone?

Henry Look, possession is nine-tenths of the law. Nobody can prove this isn't my savings.

Jean Seventy hundred and thirty-five thousand pounds!

Henry I've been frugal!

The doorbell rings

Jean God, I need a brandy. (*She goes to the sideboard and pours a large brandy*)

Henry Jean! You don't drink.

Jean I'm starting now. Henry, you'll have to tell him the truth.

Henry You're a fine one to talk with Sidney and Percy on their way to Adelaide.

Jean (*correcting him*) Adelaide and Percy on their way to Sydney. (*She drinks*)

Henry Whatever!

Jean (*referring to the drink*) God, this is awful stuff. (*She pours another brandy*)

The doorbell rings

Henry!

Henry It's only Vic and Betty. Get a grip on yourself, Jean. This is the happiest day of our lives. (*He opens the front door*)

Bill steps in

I'm afraid the dinner's off! Oh, I thought you were Vic.

Bill The clock's ticking on, you know.

Henry Clock?

Bill Taxi. On the meter.

Henry Are you Ben?

Bill I'm Bill.

Henry Ah, yes.

Bill And you're Mr Perkins, are you?

Henry I am indeed. Take that suitcase.

Jean Henry! What about that policeman?

Henry I'll deal with it.
Bill Policeman?
Henry Will you just wait outside! (*To Jean*) And you wait with him.
Jean I'm not going!
Henry Yes, you are!
Bill No, she isn't, her sister's going.

Henry glares at Bill

Henry (*to Bill*) I want her to see her sister off. Now, just take that case and go.
Jean (*to Bill*) You leave that case where it is. (*To Henry*) Henry, you're not thinking straight.
Henry Jean, stop drinking, and do as you're told!

She goes to pour herself another drink

Bill (*to Henry*) Why don't you let her sister sort out her own suitcase?
Henry (*to Bill, firmly*) Wait outside! Oh! What terminal is it?
Bill What?
Henry British Airways to Barcelona!
Bill What's that got to do with her sister flying to Sydney?
Henry Never mind! How long will it take to get there?
Bill About twenty-four hours, I imagine.
Henry To get to London Airport.
Bill At this rate about twenty-four hours.
Henry Wait outside!

Henry pushes Bill out. Still minus the suitcase

(*To Jean*) And you wait with him!
Jean I can't do it, Henry. You'll have to leave without me. (*She sits on the settee*)
Henry I'm doing no such thing! Now, come on.
Jean I can't just suddenly go off like this. I'll be a nervous wreck. It's driven me to drink already.

Henry bangs the suitcase down by the front door

Henry How many more times?! Tomorrow morning, Mr Nasty will call at the office and get my address. Mr Nasty will then come visiting 42

Elgar Avenue, and if you're still here, Mr Nasty will cut you up into very little pieces and bury you in cement.

Jean And that'll be all thanks to you.

Davenport enters from the kitchen

Henry (*pressing on, not seeing Davenport*) You silly woman!

Davenport Excuse me——

There is a brief pause while Henry decides what to do

Henry (*to Jean, lightly*) You silly woman! You silly, silly woman! (*To Davenport*) Isn't she a silly woman, mixing her drinks like this?

Davenport ignores this

Davenport I was wondering if you were ready to join me.

Henry I am indeed. After you.

Davenport They've gone then, have they?

Henry Who's that?

Davenport Your wife's sister and her husband.

Henry Ah! Mr and Mrs—er—er... (*He looks at Jean*)

Jean (*faintly*) Adelaide and Percy.

Henry I know it's *Adelaide* and *Percy*. It's Percy's second name that keeps slipping my mind. Brown! Of course. Percy Brown. What were you asking me, Sergeant?

Davenport I was asking if Mr and Mrs Brown had left for the airport.

Henry Er—not quite, no.

The doorbell rings

Jean Oh, my God!

Henry (*lightly*) You're a bundle of nerves, Jean. It's only Vic and Betty. You know what to tell them. You're giving me a surprise birthday present in *bed*!

Jean *Henry!*

The doorbell rings

God!

Henry (*to Davenport*) Look at her. I've never known her so jumpy. I hope that's not going to affect my birthday present in bed! (*He winks at Davenport and indicates for him to go into the kitchen*)

Davenport gives Henry a deadpan look and exits

Henry indicates for Jean to get rid of Vic and Betty and then hurries after Davenport into the kitchen

The doorbell rings. Jean hurries to the door and opens it

Betty comes in, carrying a wrapped present. She walks past Jean, taking her coat off

During the ensuing dialogue, she puts the present on the sideboard and Jean hurriedly puts her coat in the cupboard

Betty Sorry, we're late, darling.
Jean Oh, Betty!
Betty I say "we". That damn fool husband of mine is round the corner arguing.
Jean Arguing?
Betty We hit a taxi!
Jean A taxi?
Betty (*to Jean*) That was parked in that side street. Vic said he shouldn't have been parked right on the corner. The little taxi driver's very upset.
Jean Yes, that's Bill.
Betty Well, Bill called Vic a pillock and Vic offered to alter the shape of Bill's nose.

Jean grabs Betty

Jean Oh, Betty, it's terrible! Henry's gone mad and he's in the kitchen with a policeman.
Betty Have we missed a couple of sentences?
Jean He's stolen seven hundred and thirty-five thousand pounds.
Betty Who has?
Jean Henry! (*She grabs the briefcase and sits Betty on the settee*)
Betty (*flatly*) Henry has stolen seven hundred——

Jean Seven hundred and thirty-five thousand pounds, yes!

There is a another pause and then Betty lets out a huge guffaw

It's true. He picked up the wrong briefcase, went to the pub, saw all this money and sat on the loo overcome.

Betty Whole paragraphs seem to be disappearing now.

Jean He's booked us on the nine fifteen to Barcelona and if I don't like it there he'll buy Bali for me.

Betty You haven't taken up drinking, have you?

Jean Only since Henry came home. Gin and brandy. Betty, I don't know what to do and now the police have caught up with him.

Betty Jean! You're imagining all this. Henry couldn't possibly steal seven hundred and thirty-five thousand pounds.

Jean opens the briefcase. Betty looks down at the notes and then towards the kitchen

You sly old bugger, Henry.

Jean What the hell am I going to do?

Betty I'd take Bali.

Vic comes storming in through the front door

Vic That silly little berk is sending for the police. (*He takes off his raincoat*)

Betty What silly little berk?

Jean (*worriedly*) The police?

Vic hands the raincoat to Jean

Vic Hi, Jean. He says he's waiting to take your sister to London Airport. Do you mind if I pour myself a drink? (*He goes to the sideboard and helps himself to a drink*)

Jean puts his raincoat in the cupboard

Betty I think I need one of those, Vic. So does Jean.

Vic Jean? She doesn't drink.

Betty She does now. Brandy.

Vic Actually, I didn't know you'd got a sister.

Jean I haven't! What was that about the police?

Vic That stupid cab driver is trying to call them on that radio thing of his, says I threatened him.

Betty You did!

Jean Oh, my God!

Vic I could have sworn he said sister.

Betty It doesn't matter, Vic.

Jean (*to Vic*) He's waiting to take us to the airport.

Vic (*confused*) You to the airport? What about our dinner?!

Betty It doesn't matter, Vic. Go and apologize.

Vic Not bloody likely. He called me a pillock, the berk. Where's the birthday boy then? (*He gives Betty and Jean their drinks*)

Betty You go and apologize. They don't want any more police here tonight.

Vic I'm perfectly capable of explaining—*more* police?

Betty Henry's in the kitchen being questioned by a policeman about a robbery.

Vic Did I miss something earlier on?

Betty It's absolutely incredible, isn't it?

Vic What's poor old Henry supposed to have nicked?

Betty Seven hundred and thirty-five thousand pounds.

Vic (*to Betty*) Pounds of what?

Jean Money! It's made him go temporarily insane, Vic.

Betty I'm not surprised.

Vic Go on, pull the other one. I suppose he found it on a park bench, did he?

Jean No, on a tube train. (*She lifts the lid of the briefcase*)

Vic splutters on his drink. He picks up a bundle of the money

Henry enters from the kitchen

Henry (*calling back into the kitchen*) I won't be a moment, Sergeant. (*He closes the door*)

They rush to him, pulling him on to the settee

Jean ⎫ (*together*) ⎧ What's happened, have you been arrested?
Betty ⎭   ⎩ You haven't been arrested, have you?

Vic These aren't real, are they, Henry?

Henry snatches the bundle from Vic

Henry Jean! You shouldn't have told them.

Jean I was hoping Vic could talk some sense into you.

Henry You were supposed to take their present and show them the door.

Vic Charming!

Henry (*to Jean*) And stop drinking, will you? You're not used to it.

Jean Never mind that, what did the Sergeant say?

Betty Yes, what happened?

Henry Well, he wasn't satisfied with my explanation.

Jean I knew you should have taken it to the Lost Property office.

Betty Tell him you were going to. Tell him you didn't realize you'd got the wrong briefcase till you got home.

Vic Steady on, Betty!

Henry No. He doesn't know about the money.

Jean What?

Betty He doesn't?

Henry No.

Jean You said he wasn't satisfied with your explanation.

Henry He wasn't.

Jean Well, explanation of *what*, for goodness sake.

Henry Of my behaviour in the pub.

Vic (*referring to Henry*) What's he talking about?

Jean God only knows.

Henry The Sergeant was off duty having a drink in the pub.

Jean *The Prince of Wales*?

Henry Yes. And now he's accused me.

Betty Accused you of what?

Henry Soliciting.

Vic Soliciting?

Henry Men.

Jean (*starting to rise*) Bloody cheek, I'll go and sort——

Betty		(*sitting Jean*) No. Don't make it worse!
Vic	(*together*)	Hang on a second, Jean!
Henry		No!

Betty (*to Henry*) How could he think you were soliciting men?

Henry According to the Sergeant, I entered *The Prince of Wales* public house in a highly emotional condition and during the course of the next half-hour, he observed me going into the gentlemen's toilet three times—each time I came out looking more and more excited. He noted that I continually glanced furtively around the saloon bar, licking my lips, perspiring profusely and my eyes getting progressively more manic. Apparently I was also breathing heavily, my hands were shaking and saliva was trickling down my chin.

Jean So would his hands be shaking if he'd just been doing what you'd been doing on the loo.

Henry I wasn't going to tell him that, though, was I?! He followed me from the pub.

Vic Well, what *did* you tell him?

Henry I admitted it.

They all react

Betty You did what?

Henry I confessed.

Jean You confessed to soliciting men?!

Henry I want to get to London Airport.

Vic You'll get about as far as Wormwood Scrubs, you will!

Henry No, I won't. (*He opens the briefcase and takes out a wad of notes*) Twenty-five thousand pounds and he never saw a thing.

Jean Henry! You can't bribe a police officer.

Henry I offered ten, he asked for thirty and we settled for twenty-five.

He exits into the kitchen with the bundle of money, leaving the others astonished

Vic What's all this about London Airport?

Betty It doesn't matter, Vic!

Vic I need another drink. (*He goes to the sideboard*)

Betty I think we all do. Jean?

Jean Yes, anything to kill the pain.

Betty Doubles all round, Vic.

Jean I just can't believe this is my Henry.

Vic It's an eye-opener, all right.

Jean He's only been home five minutes and he's admitted soliciting, bribed a policeman and bought bloody Bali.

Betty And you're married to him, you lucky devil.

The doorbell rings

Jean Oh, my God!
Vic If it's that little squirt of a taxi driver——
Betty Vic, for heaven's sake!

Jean opens the front door

Bill comes storming in

Bill I can't move my taxi, you know that!
Vic You are a very silly insignificant little man.
Betty Vic, that's not a nice way to talk.
Bill No, it's bloody rude, you berk.
Jean (*to Bill*) What do you mean your taxi won't move?
Bill That twit banged my back bumper, didn't he? And my back bumper is now jammed against my rear wheel, isn't it? And my bloody taxi won't budge, will it?

Henry enters from the kitchen

Henry Would you believe it? He insists on counting it. (*To Bill*) Ah, Ben.
Jean ⎱ (*together*) Bill!
Bill ⎰
Henry Bill! Prepare to hit the track for Heathrow!
Vic What about our dinner?
Betty Vic!
Bill I'm not hitting the track for anywhere. That long streak has pranged my car.
Vic Watch it, Shorty.
Betty Vic!
Henry (*to Bill, worried*) Can't you get your taxi to start?
Bill I can get it to *start*, I can't get it to move.
Betty We'll give you a hand to straighten out your bumper.
Henry Thanks, Betty!
Vic I bloody won't. (*He points at Bill*) He phoned the police about me.
Henry The police?
Bill No, I didn't, you pillock. I couldn't get through, so I thought forget it, you berk.
Henry There you are, Vic.
Vic (*grudgingly*) That's more like it. I'll give you a hand to fix your bumper.

Betty (*to Bill, referring to Vic*) You see, he's quite a nice man, really.
Vic No, I'm not, I'm a pillock.

Vic pulls Betty out through the front door

Bill And you'd better tell your in-laws to get their skates on.
Henry Slight change of plan. The in-laws aren't going.
Bill (*surprised*) Not going?
Henry No, it's Mrs Perkins and me.
Bill She definitely said the in-laws.
Henry Well, the outlaws are going instead!

Henry pushes Bill out

(*To Jean*) Right! No more "ifs" and "buts". Fate is shining down upon us today, my girl. Get your coat!
Jean I just can't get my thoughts sorted out.
Henry Sort them out on the aeroplane. (*He takes her glass*) And leave that stuff alone. (*He gives her the briefcase*) And don't let that out of your sight. Put your coat on and wait in the taxi for me.
Jean Where are *you* going?
Henry To see if the Sergeant's finished checking his twenty-five thousand. (*He opens the kitchen door*)
Jean I can't believe you've bent a policeman.
Henry I think he was leaning a bit before I started.

Henry exits into the kitchen

Jean surveys the briefcase, then looks at the kitchen door

Jean (*tearfully*) I preferred it when you were a bit of a wimp. (*She goes to pour a drink*)

Behind her, Detective Sergeant Slater enters into the open doorway. He is wearing a raincoat and carrying a briefcase similar to the one Henry arrived with. He hesitates, then gives a little cough to attract Jean's attention

Jean drops the bottle on the tray

(*Jumping*) Ahh! (*She sees Slater*) Oh, my God!
Slater Sorry.
Jean You gave me a shock. (*She puts the briefcase behind the settee*)
Slater Are you Mrs Perkins?
Jean Er—why?
Slater May I come in please? (*He steps in and puts his briefcase down*)
Jean Well, I was just—er—what's it about? Are you selling something?
Slater No, madam.
Jean What can I do for you? It's a bit late to be calling, isn't it?
Slater Detective Sergeant Slater.
Jean Detective? Are you a policeman?
Slater Putney CID. (*He shows her his pass*)
Jean Putney?
Slater Yes, madam.
Jean Not Fulham?
Slater No. I think you'd better sit down, Mrs Perkins.
Jean No, I think I'd rather stand. Is it to do with Mr Perkins?
Slater Yes, it is. I think perhaps you'd better sit down. (*He sits Jean on the settee*)
Jean What exactly do you want to see my husband about?
Slater It's *you* I've called to see, Mrs Perkins.
Jean (*surprised*) Me?

Slater sits in the armchair

Slater Yes. I'm afraid I have some disturbing news for you.
Jean (*worriedly*) Have you?
Slater You're probably wondering why your husband isn't home.
Jean Well, I was at first, yes.
Slater We have reason to believe that Mr Perkins is dead.

Jean's face remains blank for a moment. She then looks towards the kitchen door and back to Slater

Jean (*dumbly*) Mr Perkins is dead?
Slater That's why I'm here. You'll be required to give a formal identification of the body.
Jean No, listen, Mr Perkins—my husband—I think there's been a mistake.
Slater Would you like me to make you a cup of tea, Mrs Perkins?

Jean Tea?
Slater (*rising*) Where's the kitchen?
Jean *No!* No, I'd like you to—er… What makes you think Henry's dead?
Slater Two bullet holes in the back of his head.

Jean looks to the kitchen door and back to Slater

And his body had been thrown into the river at Putney Bridge.

Jean looks to the kitchen door and back to Slater

Also his legs were tied together.
Jean His legs?
Slater And his arms.
Jean His arms.
Slater And he had weights attached to his ankles.
Jean So it wasn't an accident, then?
Slater (*slightly taken aback*) Er—no. I'm so very sorry, Mrs Perkins. I'll make you that cup of tea. (*He starts to move*)
Jean *No!* Er—er—no tea, thank you.
Slater Something stronger, perhaps, under the circumstances? Do you drink?
Jean Yes, very heavily. Brandy!

Slater reacts and pours a brandy

Help yourself.
Slater I'm on duty, Mrs Perkins.
Jean What *precisely* makes you think the body is my Henry?

Slater hands her the drink and moves to collect his briefcase

Slater Well, although he had no formal identification about his person, he was still clutching his briefcase.
Jean (*faintly*) His briefcase?
Slater Is this your husband's briefcase, Mrs Perkins? (*He holds up his briefcase*)

Jean takes a quick glance at Henry's briefcase behind the settee. She then looks at Slater's briefcase

Jean Well, it looks like it.

Slater puts the briefcase on the coffee table in front of Jean. She touches it

Oh, it's wet.

Slater It's been in the river. (*He opens the briefcase*) Are these Mr Perkins' effects? (*He takes out a pair of wet gloves and a wet scarf from the briefcase*)

Jean They would appear to be, yes.

Slater Your husband worked as an accountant in the firm of Bodley, Bodley and Crouch, is that so?

Jean Yes, in the City.

Slater 64 Fenchurch Street. (*He takes out papers from the briefcase*) There are various papers, office memos, that kind of thing, with your husband's name on them. Henry A. Perkins. Is that your husband's full name?

Jean Yes. Henry A. Perkins. Henry Alfred.

Slater And there was this personal telephone book. (*He takes out a small telephone book*)

Jean Yes, that's Henry's.

Slater And half a sandwich.

Jean Sandwich?

Slater produces a paper napkin and unwraps it

Slater Cheese and chutney, I think.

Jean Yes, he sometimes left that one.

Slater So a formal identification is required.

Jean No, that's definitely cheese and chutney.

For a moment Slater is bemused

Slater Of the body.

Jean Oh.

Slater Although there's not much doubt that it is Mr Perkins.

Jean (*looking at the kitchen*) No.

Slater We'll go in my car. Only take ten minutes. Putney Hospital.

Jean (*blankly*) Putney Hospital?

Slater He's in the mortuary there. Shall I wait here while you get your handbag?

Jean Er—well—no. No, I think I'd rather you waited in your car for a second.

Slater Will you be all right? You look a bit groggy.

Jean Yes, well, if your husband's been trussed and weighted——

Slater Of course. Is there anyone else in the house?

Jean (*taken aback*) What?

Slater To look after you?

Jean Well—er—(*then brightly*) yes! I've got my sister staying.

Slater Sister? That's good.

Jean Yes. Adelaide. They're upstairs. She and her husband. Adelaide and—er—Percy.

Slater They'll be able to keep an eye on you, then.

Jean Yes.

Slater Well, I'll wait in the car while you tell your sister the sad news about your husband.

Henry comes in from the kitchen

Henry Would you believe it? Hundred and fifty short. (*He sees Slater*) Oh.

Jean (*hoarsely*) Ah! Yes. Good Lord! This gentleman is a policeman.

Henry takes a quick look back at the kitchen

Henry Policeman? (*Then lightly*) From Fulham?

Slater Putney, actually.

Henry Putney?

Slater Detective Sergeant Slater.

Jean He's brought some very disturbing news. I don't think I know how to handle it.

Henry Well, you just sit down, Jean.

Jean No, I'm better standing, I can get to the drinks more easily. (*She moves to the sideboard and starts to pour herself another glass*)

Henry Well, what seems to be the trouble, Sergeant? I'm Mr Perkins.

Jean drops her glass on the tray with a crash. Henry and Slater turn. Jean smiles

Slater Mr Perkins?

Henry Correct.

Slater You're a relative are you, sir?
Henry Relative of who?
Slater Of Mr Henry Alfred Perkins.
Henry I am——
Jean (*cutting in*) Yes, he is! He's a relative. He's Henry's brother. (*She comes down with her drink. She is now getting tipsy*)

Henry's face goes blank

Henry (*flatly*) Henry's brother.
Jean Yes! This is my poor Henry's brother!
Slater Oh. Well, I'm afraid I have a shock for you, Mr Perkins.
Henry Yes, I was beginning to think you might have.
Slater (*to Jean*) Shall I tell him or will you?
Jean I think it's going to be a shock whoever tells him.
Slater We have every reason to believe that Mr Henry Perkins is dead.

Henry takes this in

Henry Yes, that's a shock all right.
Jean He's been murdered.

Henry takes this in

Henry Has he?
Slater That would appear to fit the facts of the case, sir.
Jean Foul play.
Slater We took his body out of the Thames. Two bullet wounds in the back of his head.
Jean And he's been trussed up and weighted down.
Henry Yes, that's foul play all right. (*At a loss*) How exactly—er—why exactly——
Jean (*pointedly*) All he had with him was his *briefcase*.
Henry His—er...?

Slater holds out his briefcase

Slater This is your brother's briefcase, Mr Perkins?
Henry (*realizing*) Ah! Oo! Yes, that certainly looks like my poor brother Henry's briefcase.

Jean It's all wet.

Henry Oh dear, oh dear, oh dear.

Slater And as Mrs Perkins is the next of kin we need her to make a positive identification of the body.

Henry The body that was found in the Thames?

Slater Yes.

Henry Yes, that'll be Mr Nasty, er, nasty, very nasty.

Jean (*clutching Henry's arm*) Henry!

Henry sits her on the settee

Henry (*quickly*) You can't call Henry back, Jean! If Henry's gone to Heaven, he's gone to Heaven. You'll have to rely on me now. His little brother—Freddy. (*To Slater*) You'll have to excuse my wife. (*He realizes what he's said*) Yes—you'll have to excuse my wife. (*Looking around*) I don't know where she's got to. I know she would have liked to have been here to comfort Jean ... but—er—Genevieve—that's my wife... Genevieve must be lying down resting. Before she and I depart for Sydney.

Slater Sydney, eh, you're a long way from home.

Henry Yes, the wife and I—that's Genevieve—we've been over here on holiday. Makes a change from the old farm back home. Not so many sheep in Fulham. (*To Jean*) Well, poor old Henry! This is going to be a hell of a shock to Genevieve.

Jean Yes. We've got to tell Adelaide and Percy as well, Freddy.

Henry Yes, them too! Well, this will put the family arrangements right up the spout, won't it? (*To Slater*) Tell you what! I think we all need a quick cup of tea. You wait in the—er... (*He looks at the kitchen and hesitates*) No! You wait in the dining-room, will you?

Slater Cup of tea certainly won't do Mrs Perkins any harm.

Jean (*rising*) I'd prefer a whisky. (*She crosses to the sideboard to pour herself another drink*)

Slater One bright spot, Mrs Perkins, is that so many of your family were here at this time.

Jean That is a comfort, yes.

The kitchen door opens and Davenport pops his head out

Davenport I'm waiting. One hundred and fifty!

Davenport retreats, closing the door

There is a pause as Henry considers the situation

Henry (*finally, to Slater*) That's my other brother.

Jean drops her glass on the drinks tray with a crash

Slater Other brother?

Henry Yes, that's Archie. Archie's waiting for me to go back and finish playing darts—one hundred and fifty! (*He chuckles*) Oh, Archie's good.

Jean Henry!

Henry It's no good calling him! (*He sits Jean on the settee*)

Jean Henry!

Henry I'm Freddy. (*To Slater*) She just can't accept he's gone. (*To Jean*) It's me, Freddy, Henry's brother, Freddy Perkins. Poor old Henry's dead but Freddy and Genevieve will look after you.

Jean What are we going to do?!

Henry We're going to pray, that's what we're going to do. *Pray*—very, very hard—for Henry. (*To Slater*) You wait in there. While Mrs Perkins and I are making the tea we'll tell Archie the sad news about Henry.

Jean Oh, God.

Henry And Archie can tell Percy and Adelaide.

Jean Oh, God.

Henry And Percy and Adelaide can tell Genevieve.

Jean Oh, God!

Slater is looking confused

Henry (*to Slater*) It's all right, you don't have to tell anybody.

Slater goes into the dining-room with his briefcase, looking bewildered

Jean (*rising*) This is catastrophic!

Henry It's nothing of the sort. It's a double bonus.

Jean A double bonus?!

Henry If "Henry Perkins" has been shot, trussed and drowned, then nobody will ever come looking for him living the life of luxury in the foothills of Barcelona.

Jean What's the other bonus?

Henry As it's *Mr Nasty* who has been shot, trussed and drowned, Mr Nasty can't come after us.

Jean No, but whoever did the shooting, trussing and drowning *can*.

Henry You always look on the black side. Right! Let's get rid of brother Archie first.

Jean Brother Archie?

Henry Sergeant Davenport, that bent copper. He's one hundred and fifty pounds short. (*Looking around*) Here, where's my briefcase with the money? (*He sees it behind the settee*) Ah! (*He picks up the briefcase*)

Jean You should have told the truth from the beginning.

Henry You keep saying that, but you're the one who invented Adelaide and Percy, then killed me off and then made me christen myself Freddy!

The telephone rings. Henry and Jean look at each other. Henry indicates for Jean to pick it up. She does so while Henry removes three fifty pound notes from the briefcase

Jean (*into the phone, apprehensively*) Hello? ... What? ... I can't follow what you're saying.

Henry Who is it?

Jean I don't know. He's foreign.

Henry Foreign? (*He grabs the phone. Into the phone*) Hello?! ... Will you speak English, please? ... Look, if this is some kind of obscene telephone call... What? ... What? (*To Jean*) Just keeps saying "brerfcurse".

Jean Brerfcurse?

Henry "Brerfcurse, brerfcurse".

Jean Briefcase!

Henry What?

Jean He's saying "briefcase".

Henry looks aghast

Henry (*into the phone*) Sorry, wrong number! (*He bangs the phone down*)

Jean That must be Mr Big.

Henry Mr Big?

Jean The one who's done away with Mr Nasty.

Henry How the hell did he get our telephone number?

Jean Where do you think? From your bloody "brerfcurse"!

Henry (*pointing to the dining-room*) But Sergeant Slater's got that.

Jean But who had it first? Mr Nasty delivered your briefcase to Mr Big. Mr Big opens it, expecting to find seven hundred and thirty-five thousand pounds, and instead of which he sees a cheese and chutney sandwich and your telephone book. (*She hurries to pour herself a drink*)

Henry You're right. That's what must have happened.

Vic comes through the front door

Vic Right!

Jean (*yelling*) Ahhh! (*She drops the glass on to the tray with a crash*)

Henry Vic!

Vic We've fixed Bill's bumper.

Henry Great! (*To Jean*) Come on. (*He picks up his briefcase*)

Jean Come on? Where to?

Henry London Airport, for God's sake.

Jean You can't go now!

Henry Now's a damn good time, if you ask me.

Jean I can't go either. (*She points to the dining-room*) That other Police Sergeant's waiting for me.

Vic What "other" Police Sergeant?

Henry Never mind, Vic.

Jean We've got one in the kitchen and one in the dining-room.

Vic One in the kitchen and one...?

Henry Never mind, Vic!

Jean (*to Henry*) I've got to go to the mortuary.

Vic Go to the mortuary?

Henry (*to Vic*) Vic! (*To Jean*) You're coming to Barcelona with me! (*To Vic*) Give the one in the kitchen his one hundred and fifty pounds. (*He puts the one hundred and fifty pounds in Vic's top pocket*)

Vic I thought it was twenty-five thousand.

Henry It is! He's one hundred and fifty pounds short. Just give it to him. (*He pushes Vic towards the kitchen*)

Jean (*to Henry*) But who's going to identify the dead body?

Vic stops

Vic Dead body?!

Henry Vic!

Vic What dead body?

Jean Mr Nasty's been found in the river, his arms and legs tied together with rope, weights round his ankles and two gaping bullet wounds in the back of his head.

Henry Jean, you are not the *News of the World!* Vic, just give that Sergeant his hundred and fifty and then you and Betty get home as fast as you can. You haven't been here tonight, you haven't seen anything, you don't know anything.

Vic You can say that again.

Henry *(to Jean)* You wait outside and I'll get your coat. *(He goes to open the cupboard)*

The phone rings. Henry and Jean freeze

(To Vic in urgent whisper) Don't answer it!

Vic *(whispering)* I wasn't going to.

The phone continues to ring

Why aren't *you* answering it?

Jean It's *him.*

Vic Who?

Henry Mr Nasty.

Vic I thought Mr Nasty was in the river.

Jean *(correcting Henry)* It's not Mr Nasty, it's Mr Big!

Henry Oh, yes, I meant Mr Big.

Vic Do I know Mr Big?

Henry Mr Brerfcurse.

Vic Who?

Jean He's foreign.

Vic Who is?

Henry Mr Brerfcurse.

Jean Mr Briefcase!

Vic Who the hell's Mr Brief—*(yelling)—case!*

Henry }
Jean } *(together)* Sssssh!

Vic How the hell did he get your telephone number?

Henry Via my cheese and chutney sandwich, never mind!

Jean I knew this would happen! (*She breaks down in tears and sits in the armchair*)

Henry and Vic go to her. Henry puts his briefcase down R *of the armchair*

Henry ⎱ (*together*) ⎰ Don't start that again, please!
Vic ⎰   ⎱ Easy does it, Jean.
Vic I'll get her a brandy.
Henry Don't give her any more, for heaven's sake!

Vic pours a brandy

Betty enters from the front door

Betty Come on, Bill's waiting! (*She sees Jean*) What's the matter with Jean?
Vic She's having hysterics.
Henry She's drunk.
Vic That too.
Betty God! (*She picks up the telephone which has been ringing throughout. Into the phone*) Hello?
Henry No! Betty! (*He drops Jean, who slips to the floor, as he hurries to Betty*) Put that down!
Betty (*to Henry*) Sssh! (*Into the phone*) I beg your pardon? (*Into the phone*) Brerfcurse?

Henry grabs the receiver and slams it down

(*To Henry*) That's not very nice.
Henry You don't have to be nice to Mr Nasty.
Vic I thought Mr Nasty had been trussed and weighted.
Henry He was! I meant Mr Big!
Betty Who's Mr Big?
Henry The one who trussed and weighted Mr Nasty.
Vic It's Mr Brerfcurse!
Betty Mr Who?

Henry glares at Vic who takes the drink to Jean

Henry Mr Briefcase!

Betty Oh, bloody hell! What exactly's happened to Mr Nasty?

Jean looks up

Jean (*wailing*) Mr Big put him in the river.
Henry Jean!
Betty Mr Big put him in the...?
Jean Two bullets in the back of his head!
Betty Good God!
Vic (*to Jean*) Drink this. (*He holds out the glass*)
Betty (*taking the drink*) Thanks. (*She takes a swig*)

The phone rings. They all freeze. Jean pulls herself up into the armchair

Jean Henry! Tell him you'll give him back his money.
Henry No way!
Betty Besides, it's twenty-five thousand short now.
Henry Yes, I'd probably get kneecapped just for that.
Vic Offer to pay the twenty-five back.
Henry What, over the next twenty-five years?
Jean He'll understand. Tell him you'll give it back.
Vic She's right, old man. It's all getting a bit hot now. A dead body, two
   police forces and a foreign Mr Brerfcurse.

Henry hesitates and then picks up the phone

   Well done!
Jean Thank God!
Henry (*into the phone*) And the same to you! (*He replaces the receiver*)
Jean Henry!
Vic (*to Henry*) Mr Big won't like that!
Betty Good for you, Henry!
Jean Betty!
Vic (*to Betty*) This is nothing to do with us. This is between Henry and Mr
   Big. (*He collects his and Betty's coats*)
Henry I've been given this opportunity and I'm grabbing it with both
   hands.
Vic Betty, give Henry his present. (*To Jean*) Thanks for a lovely evening.
   And thanks for a delicious dinner.

Betty We haven't had any dinner.
Vic Good. We'll pick up a take-away on the way home and watch telly.

Vic exits through the front door

Betty Watch the telly?! We've got *Crimewatch* for real here. (*She sits on the arm of the armchair*)
Henry Betty, go with Vic. You'd better get home, for God's sake.

The phone rings. They freeze

Davenport enters from the kitchen

Davenport You seem to be taking——

Henry, without thinking, sits on Betty's lap. Davenport stops and looks at them. They all smile and attempt to appear nonchalant. Davenport looks at the ringing telephone and their smiles drop. He looks back at them— they smile. He lifts the receiver

(*Into the phone*) Perkins residence.
Jean (*nearly fainting*) Ahh! (*She slips to the floor again*)
Davenport (*into the phone*) Pardon? (*To Henry*) Anybody here called Brerfcurse?

Henry thinks

Henry I don't think so, no.
Davenport (*into the phone*) You get in touch with directory enquiries. (*He replaces the receiver. To Betty*) I don't believe we've met, madam. Detective Sergeant Davenport, Fulham CID.
Betty (*pointedly*) Oh, yes. I've heard about you.
Davenport (*smiling*) All good, I hope?
Betty Patchy.
Davenport (*still smiling, to Henry*) I was expecting you back in the kitchen, Mr Perkins—with the rest of your "charitable contribution".
Henry Oh, yes. (*He looks to the front door*) He went out with it. (*To Davenport*) Just wait in the kitchen, I'll get some more.
Davenport Oh! You must have quite a stash of cash hidden away, Mr Perkins.

Henry Nothing of the sort.

The front door opens and Bill walks in

Bill Is *anybody* going to London Airport tonight?
Henry Ah, it's Ben.
Bill It's *Bill*! And someone's going to get a bloody big one at the end of today. Now is it you, the in-laws, or the outlaws?
Jean It's nobody!
Bill Nobody?
Henry Yes, it is. It's Mr and Mrs Brown.
Bill Mr and Mrs Brown?
Henry Yes.
Bill Where did they come from?
Henry They're our in-laws!
Bill So it's not *you*, then.
Henry No! Wait outside!
Bill How long for?
Henry For as long as it takes!
Bill I'm not hanging about much longer. Five minutes, then I'm off.
Henry They'll be less than five minutes. Now, take Mr and Mrs Brown's suitcase! (*He hands Bill the suitcase*)
Bill What, just the one?
Henry Yes!
Bill And they've come all the way from Australia?
Henry Yes!
Bill What *are* your in-laws, nudists?

Bill exits with the suitcase

Henry (*to Davenport; lightly*) Damn taxi drivers.
Davenport He's got a point though, hasn't he? Two people—round the world trip—one suitcase. (*To Jean*) *Are* Mr and Mrs Brown nudists, Mrs Perkins?
Jean (*laughing foolishly*) Only when they take their clothes off.

Henry lifts Jean

Henry Mrs Perkins is getting upset.

Jean Mrs Perkins is getting drunk.

Henry She's not used to alcohol.

Jean But she's learning fast. (*She moves up to the sideboard*)

Henry (*to Davenport*) Adelaide and she are very close and Australia is such a long way off.

Davenport I somehow thought that maybe it was *you* and *Mrs Perkins* who were planning a sudden little trip abroad.

Henry Us?

Davenport Taxi driver seemed to think that it was a possibility, too.

Henry No, no.

Davenport You'd need a lot of cash for a trip like that.

Henry No. We don't want to go abroad, do we, Jean?

Jean I bloody don't! (*She sits in the armchair with her drink*)

Henry No, we're staying here. It's Mr and Mrs Brown who are going to Sydney. Back to the sheep farm and the jolly old clippers. (*He smiles at Davenport*)

Davenport So where are they, then? Your in-laws?

Henry Mr and Mrs Brown? Percy and Adelaide? Well—er——

Betty (*interrupting*) Well, Percy's outside, isn't he, Henry?

Henry Thanks for reminding me. Yes, Percy is outside and—er——

Betty (*interrupting*) And I'm Adelaide.

Henry looks blankly at Betty

Jean's sister from Sydney.

Henry (*pleased*) Yes!

Jean (*hysterically*) Sister from Sydney!

Jean runs upstairs

The other three watch as she and her hysterics disappear along the landing

Henry (*to Davenport*) She's been like that all day. (*To Betty*) She'll be inconsolable when you've gone, Adelaide. (*To Davenport*) Well, there we are. You've met Mrs Brown.

Davenport And what about your husband?

Henry Oh no, you don't want to meet Mr Brown.

Vic enters through the front door

Vic (*to Betty*) Look, I've been waiting for you outside! (*He grabs Betty's arm, but stops on seeing Davenport*)

Henry Talk of the devil! The very man! You ask where he is and lo and behold! We were just talking about you—(*he adopts an Australian accent*) me ol' bluey-sport-digger.

Vic (*bemused*) Blue-sport-digger?

Henry Indeed we were, me and the—(*he indicates Davenport*) gentleman *from the kitchen.*

Vic (*realizing*) Oh, the kitchen!

Henry Yes! One hundred and fifty. (*He takes the one hundred and fifty pounds from Vic's top pocket*) Thank you. (*He puts the money in Davenport's pocket*) There we are, that makes up the shortfall. Twenty five thou'! (*He pulls Davenport across him towards the front door. To Davenport*) Careful how you cross the road.

Davenport (*to Vic*) You have a safe journey then, Mr Brown. (*He waits for Vic to reply*)

Henry looks to Vic. Vic looks around for "Mr Brown"

Henry (*in Vic's ear*) Mr Brown!

Vic still looks bemused

Betty He's a bit deaf.

Vic Deaf?

Betty moves to Vic

Betty (*louder*) Yes, dear, we know. (*Even louder*) He said have a safe journey!

Vic (*nonplussed*) Oh, thanks.

Davenport (*to Betty*) After you, Mrs Brown.

Vic Mrs...?!

Henry (*goosing Vic*) Brown!

Vic reacts to his bottom being pinched by Henry

Betty (*to Vic*) Come on, Percy!

Vic is even more confused

Vic Am I hearing straight?

Henry Not yet, but you will after the operation. (*He shakes Vic's hand. Loudly*) It's been a lovely visit.

Vic Is Jean still in a bit of a state?

Henry Yes, she is!

Betty (*shouting*) Jean's upstairs and she's very, very upset about us leaving. (*She moves to the front door*)

Vic (*to Henry*) Well, maybe we should stay then.

Henry Don't be daft! You've got to get back to the farm. Go on!

Vic The farm?

Henry The farm!

Davenport (*to Vic; loudly*) Sydney!

Vic (*dumbly*) Oh, pleased to meet you. (*He offers his hand to Davenport*)

Henry pulls him away

Henry (*to Davenport*) I can see this sad farewell is going to be prolonged. You'd better leave us to it.

Davenport takes the bundle from his raincoat pocket and adds the one hundred and fifty pounds from his top pocket

Davenport Yes, right. And thanks, Mr Perkins, it's been a most *rewarding* little visit.

Henry A pleasure.

Davenport (*To Vic; very loudly*) I hope you find your sheep in good shape.

Davenport exits

Henry (*relieved*) Thank God! He's gone!

Vic Would anybody mind if I went out and came back in again?

Henry pulls Vic across to the front door

Henry It doesn't matter, Vic. Take him home, Betty. (*He calls upstairs*) Come on, Jean! We're off! (*He picks up the briefcase from* R *of the armchair*)

The dining-room door opens and Slater appears, still carrying his briefcase

Slater Excuse me—I think you said something about a cup of tea, Mr Perkins.

Vic (*to Slater*) You're new around here, aren't you?

Henry drops his briefcase by the stairs and fulsomely hurries to Slater

Henry (*to Slater*) I'm so sorry! Tea's on its way. (*To Vic and Betty*) This gentleman is from the dining-room.

Henry turns Slater around, and pushes him back into the dining-room

Vic Betty, let's go home while we're reasonably sane.

Vic exits out of the front door

Jean comes unsteadily downstairs in her nightie

Betty Jean! What the hell are you up to?

Jean Getting a glass of hot milk and several aspirins! (*She moves towards the kitchen*)

Henry and Betty grab her

Betty You'll make yourself ill, you've been drinking!

Jean Good idea. (*She picks up the brandy bottle and heads towards the kitchen*)

Henry grabs her

Henry And what the dickens are you doing in your dressing-gown?

Jean I'm going to bed! (*She surveys the bottle*) Somebody's been at my brandy.

Henry Jean! You have two choices and bed isn't one of them.

Betty What's her two choices?

Henry Barcelona or the mortuary.

Betty (*to Jean*) She's taking Barcelona.

Jean (*to Betty*) Will you stop trying to run my life for me?!

Betty Well, *you* obviously don't know which direction to take. (*To Henry*) Why would Jean have to go to the mortuary?

Henry Never mind!

Jean Because Sergeant Slater thinks Mr Nasty's body is Henry!

Betty What? (*To Henry*) Does Vic know about this added complication?

Henry God knows what Vic knows, but don't confuse him any more.

Vic comes storming through the door

Vic Betty! Are you coming home or not?!

Betty I'm trying to sort out these two.

Jean "These two" don't need sorting out. (*She points to Henry*) He's going to Barcelona and I'm going to bed.

Vic Barcelona? Bed?

Henry It's Barcelona with me or Sergeant Slater with dead Mr Nasty.

Vic Blimey! You walk out the door in this place and when you come back you're in cuckoo-land.

Henry Vic, please! Go home!

Jean (*gaily*) Yes, the happy birthday celebrations are over.

Betty Jean, you're well on the way to getting sloshed.

Jean Betty, I've already arrived. (*To Henry*) I'm getting an aspirin and I'm sleeping in the spare room.

Henry grabs the blanket

Henry You're sleeping with me in Barcelona.

Jean Find yourself a bull and sleep with that!

Jean exits into the kitchen with the brandy bottle, leaving Henry clutching the blanket

Betty runs towards the kitchen

Betty Jean! (*She stops*) Vic, even with a satellite dish you couldn't get better than this.

Betty exits into the kitchen

Henry throws the blanket on the settee

Henry If Jean makes us miss that aeroplane—— (*He grabs his briefcase*)

Vic Jean isn't going, Henry!

Henry moves towards the kitchen

Henry Oh, yes she is. Vic, go and make sure that taxi driver doesn't push
off. You give him fifty pounds and tell him to wait. (*He sits on the right
end of the settee*)
Vic I'm getting Betty and taking her home.

Henry grabs Vic

Henry I'll get Betty, you go and see Ben.
Vic It's Bill.

Henry sits Vic on the left end of the settee and puts the briefcase on his lap

Henry Bill, Ben, whoever he is! (*He opens the briefcase*) Give him fifty
pounds and tell him he's not to leave without us. (*He makes to peel off
a fifty pound note*)

Davenport enters through the front door

Davenport Right! Where's Mr Perkins, then?

*As Davenport turns to close the front door, Henry bangs the lid of the
briefcase shut, pulls the blanket from the arm of the settee and throws it
over himself and Vic. The blanket is up to their necks and their hands are
beneath the blanket. Davenport turns back into the room and reacts on
seeing Henry and Vic under the blanket. He walks slowly over to them. Vic
worried, looks to Henry. Henry looks blank. They both look back at
Davenport who suddenly grins broadly and, naughtily, wags his finger at
them*

Henry We weren't expecting you back, Sergeant.
Davenport Is that why you're looking so guilty?
Henry Guilty? Us? We're not looking guilty, are we, Percy?
Vic No, we're not looking guilty, Henry.
Henry We're just sitting here, aren't we, Percy?
Vic That's right, Henry. Relaxing.

Henry Yes. Under the blanket. Having a little—(*he is at a loss*) a little—
er...

Davenport A little what, Mr Perkins?

Henry Well—er—you know.

Davenport No, I don't, Mr Perkins.

Henry Well, *we* know, don't we, Percy?

Vic Know what?

Henry What we're doing on the settee. Under the blanket. (*He smiles at Davenport*)

Davenport I see.

Vic Well, I don't.

Henry It's all right, Percy. He knows what you get up to on the farm—
when you're away from home for weeks on end—with no company but
your sheep.

Vic tries to work it out

Vic (*suddenly realizing*) Ohhh!

Henry Yes!

Davenport You're having quite a busy evening, Mr Perkins.

Henry Yes, it's been my lucky night, hasn't it? So what can we do for you,
Sergeant? We're in a bit of a hurry.

Davenport Is that a fact, now?

Henry Yes, it is. Mr Brown is very keen to get on an aeroplane.

Davenport Is that a new position, is it?

Henry No! Can we be of any assistance to you, Sergeant?

Davenport Well, I'm not quite sure, Mr Perkins. I'm trying to piece it all
together.

Henry You don't want to do that, does he, Percy?

Vic Definitely not, Henry.

Davenport (*to Vic*) I actually returned to tell you about your taxi driver,
Mr Brown.

Henry (*worriedly*) Bill?

Davenport He's driven off.

Henry (*worriedly*) Driven off?

Davenport In a bit of a huff.

Henry (*worriedly*) A huff?

Davenport (*to Henry*) You seem very worried about your brother-in-
law's taxi, Mr Perkins.

Henry Well, I know how anxious he is to get back—it's the lambing season, isn't it, Percy?

Vic *(confused)* Is it?

Henry Percy! *(To Davenport)* Why's Bill driven off in a huff?

Davenport Said you'd been messing him about.

Henry Damn cheek.

Davenport *(to Vic)* He left your suitcase on the pavement, Mr Brown.

Vic What suitcase?

Henry closes his eyes

Henry The little suitcase containing your boomerang and didgeridoo, Percy.

Vic *(blankly)* Oh, *that* suitcase.

Davenport Yes, you travel light because you and your wife are nudists.

Vic Nudists?!

Henry We explained it's only when you've got no clothes on, Percy.

Vic considers this

Vic God, I wish I'd stayed in bed this morning.

Davenport I'll bring your suitcase in, Mr Brown.

Henry No, don't trouble yourself. *(To Vic)* You want it left outside, don't you.

Vic How do *I* know what I want?

Henry *(to Davenport)* Please! Don't bother.

Davenport OK. Suit yourself. Isn't it getting a bit steamy under that blanket?

Davenport winks at them and exits through the front door

They throw the blanket off

Vic Oh, my God!

Henry Oh, shut up, Vic, it could have been worse.

Vic Worse?! That Police Sergeant thinks I'm a pervert.

Henry Just be grateful he didn't make a pass at you. Now, look, I'll grab Jean and we'll go out the back way. Right, give me the keys to your car.

Vic My car? What for?

Henry To get to the airport. Our driver's pushed off, hasn't he?

Vic I'm not giving you my car.

Henry Well, I don't own one, do I?

Vic I like that car.

Henry Five thousand pounds.

Vic Ten.

Henry Seven and a half.

Vic Done.

They shake hands and Henry opens the briefcase

Betty enters from the kitchen

Betty Henry!

Henry (*jumping*) Ah! (*He goes to shut the briefcase, but realizes it's Betty*) Oh, it's you, Betty!

Betty Jean's getting quietly plastered in there.

Henry You should have taken that brandy away from her.

Betty She's finished the brandy, she's on the cooking sherry now.

Henry Silly woman!

Betty She's determined to stay, Henry. She says she doesn't want to go First Class to Barcelona or anywhere else.

Henry Silly woman!!

Vic First Class to the Old Bailey, that's what I'll get.

Betty The Old Bailey?

Vic Henry's just told that bent copper that he's having it off with me here and I'm having it off with the sheep in Sydney!

Betty Henry! What made you say a thing like that?

Henry It seemed like a good idea at the time. (*To Vic*) I'll give you your seven and a half thousand.

Betty What's that for?

Henry His car. (*He opens the briefcase*)

Betty sits beside Vic

Betty Seven and a half thousand?! (*To Vic*) The garage told you they wouldn't give you five hundred for it.

Henry Five hundred?!

Vic (*shrugging*) It's a seller's market.

Henry starts to give Vic the money

Slater appears from the dining-room, still carrying his briefcase

Slater Excuse me, is that tea——?

Henry stuffs the money back in the briefcase and quickly pulls the blanket over the three of them. Under the blanket, Henry locks the briefcase. Slater puts his briefcase on the right side of the armchair and walks over to them, bemused by what he sees

(*To Henry*) Maybe we should forget about the tea. Just get your sister-in-law, will you, sir.
Henry Actually, Sergeant, Mrs Perkins is still trying to pull herself together.

Betty slides out from under the blanket

Betty Why don't I help Mrs Perkins make the tea, Sergeant?
Henry Now, that's a very good idea, Adelaide.
Vic (*confused*) Adelaide?
Henry (*pointedly*) Adelaide!
Slater (*brightly*) Adelaide? So, you're Mrs Perkins' sister, are you?
Vic Sister?
Henry Sister!
Slater (*to Vic*) And I take it you're this lady's husband?
Vic I think that still holds, yes.
Betty Yes. (*To Slater*) My husband and I are from Sydney.
Vic Sydney?
Henry Oh, my God! (*He buries his head*)
Slater (*to Vic*) That's a coincidence!
Vic Why, are *you* from Sydney?

Henry looks up

Henry No, *I* am!

Vic looks totally confused

Vic You're from Sydney?

Henry You know I am! Me and my wife.
Vic Ah! Now I know your wife. Jean.
Henry (*quickly jumping in*) Genevieve.

Vic tries to assimilate this

Vic (*realizing*) Oh, Genevieve!
Betty There's no need to burst into song, Percy! I'll make the tea.

Betty smiles sweetly and exits into the kitchen

Vic (*to Henry*) Could I just clarify something about Genevieve?
Henry Not now!
Slater I suppose you all flew over from Sydney together, did you? (*He turns to pick up his briefcase*)

Henry surreptitiously puts his briefcase by the right end of the settee and stands

Henry That's correct. Percy and Adelaide. Me and Genevieve.
Slater (*to Vic*) And do you have a farm as well?
Vic As well as what?

Henry moves to Slater

Henry As well as me, Percy! (*To Slater*) There's a bit of rivalry between us. The Browns and the Perkins. In-laws, you know. Percy being married to the sister of my brother's wife.
Slater I understand.
Henry Do you? Good. Percy, why don't you go and help Adelaide make the tea?
Vic Henry!
Henry No, no, I told you, you weren't to mention that name, Percy.
Vic What name, Henry?
Henry *That* name, Percy. I might break down and weep! (*To Slater*) I'd be grateful if you'd leave us alone in our hour of sorrow.
Vic Henry!
Henry (*cutting in*) No! No! No! No! It's too fresh, Percy.
Vic What's fresh, Henry?

Henry No, Henry's not fresh. Not any more. (*To Slater*) Will you please wait in the dining-room?

Slater (*referring to Vic*) He does know, doesn't he?

Henry Yes, he knows! I've told him!

Vic Told me what?

Slater That Henry Perkins is dead.

Henry Oh, my God! (*He slumps in the armchair*)

Vic is totally baffled and attempts to assimilate this latest piece of information

Vic (*finally*) How do you mean, dead?

Slater (*to Henry*) I thought you said you'd told him?

Henry looks up

Henry Yes, but I'd only got as far as Henry not looking too well.

Slater (*to Vic*) His body was found under Putney Bridge.

Vic (*blankly*) Putney Bridge?

Slater In the river.

Vic looks across to Henry

Vic (*to Henry*) Do I know about the river?

Henry Yes, I told you. (*To Slater*) But I'd only got as far as Henry not looking too well.

Vic (*still not realizing*) Henry—in the river?

Henry I told you he was trussed up and shot—(*to Slater*) and not looking too well.

Vic (*realizing*) Oh! Trussed up and...?!

Henry Yes!

Vic That would explain why he wasn't looking too well.

Henry (*to Slater*) I was trying to break it to Percy gently. (*To Vic*) They identified Henry by his briefcase. (*He indicates the briefcase which Slater is holding*)

Vic Ah, yes! His "brerfcurse".

Slater looks bemused. Henry looks pained

Henry That's right. Poor old Henry. That's all he had with him. A few papers, his diary and half a cheese and chutney sandwich.

Vic Dear, oh dear, oh dear. Poor Jean must be knocked sideways.
Henry Yes!
Slater Luckily, her brother-in-law was here at the time. (*He indicates Henry*)
Henry Oh, my God! (*He collapses in the chair*)
Vic I thought *I* was her brother-in-law.

Henry rises and angrily goes to Vic

Henry You are! So am I! Only we're from different sides of the family. You're married to Jean's sister, Adelaide, and I'm the brother of Jean's late husband, Henry.

Vic takes this in

Vic That's something else I know, isn't it?
Henry (*turning to Slater*) Now you can see why I had to break it to him slowly. He hasn't been the same since he fell off that kangaroo in Queensland. (*To Vic*) Jean has two brothers-in-law. You, Percy, and me—good old reliable Freddy.

Vic thinks for a second

Vic (*brightly*) Ah!! "Good old reliable Freddy", got it! You're reliable Freddy, I'm Australian Percy and Henry's dead, right?
Henry Right!
Vic And we're both brother-in-laws to Jean, yes?
Henry Yes!
Slater And so's Archie.
Henry Oh, my God! (*He collapses on the settee next to Vic*)
Vic Archie?
Henry I'd forgotten about Archie.
Vic (*blankly*) And he's a brother-in-law as well, is he, Freddy?
Henry Yes. "Not so reliable Archie".
Vic (*at a loss*) Not so reliable Archie?
Slater Did Archie come over from Sydney, as well?

There is a pause

Henry No, he didn't, did he, Percy?

Vic I don't think he did, no. He's from—er——
Henry He's from—er——

Vic and Henry look at each other

Henry ⎱ *(together)* ⎰ Manchester.
Vic ⎰   ⎱ The Falkland Islands.
Henry Archie's a travelling salesman.
Slater I suppose that's what makes him so unreliable.
Vic ⎱ *(together)* ⎰ Yes, 'fraid so.
Henry ⎰   ⎱ Yes, yes, yes.
Vic While we're on the subject of Archie——
Henry *(cutting in)* We're not, Percy. Unreliable Archie has gone now—
he's taken his samples up to Manchester and he's not coming back.

Davenport enters, carrying the suitcase

Davenport Here we are!

*Henry and Vic exchange a blank look. Henry goes over to Davenport and
warmly shakes his hand*

Henry *(gaily, to Davenport)* He's come back! *(To the others)* Would you
believe it—he is back!
Davenport Well, I thought I shouldn't go——
Henry *(cutting in)* And we're glad you didn't. *(At a loss)* Isn't that terrific,
Percy?

Vic can only nod

Yes, terrific!
Davenport I was half-way down the road and I thought I can't leave that
suitcase on the pavement.
Henry Certainly not! So he came back for it. Great!

Davenport moves to Vic

Davenport *(to Vic)* There we are. One suitcase.
Vic *(expansively)* Thank you, Archie!

Davenport hesitates and then slowly looks to Henry, who holds his head in his hands. Curtain music begins to play

CURTAIN

ACT II

The action is continuous

Davenport I beg your pardon?

Vic I said "thank you, Archie".

Henry We know what you said, Percy. (*To Slater, gaily*) Unreliable Archie is back!

Slater Not so unreliable after all.

Henry No. (*He kisses Davenport warmly on the cheek*)

Davenport looks suitably surprised

   Oh, Archie!

Davenport Archie?

Henry Oh, Archie, you haven't actually met this gentleman, have you? (*He indicates Slater*)

Davenport (*blankly*) No.

Henry Good! (*Pointedly*) This is Detective Sergeant Slater. (*He pulls Davenport across him to Slater*)

Slater How do you do.

Davenport (*surprised*) Are you a Police Officer?

Henry I thought you'd be surprised, Archie.

Slater Putney CID.

Davenport Putney, eh?

Henry (*referring to Davenport*) And this is Archie. Archie *Perkins*. (*He pats Davenport's cheek affectionately*)

Davenport's face remains expressionless, then he breaks into a grin

Davenport Archie Perkins.

Henry (*brightly*) My big brother. (*He pats Davenport's cheek affectionately*)

Davenport Your big brother.

Henry (*indicating Vic*) And his big brother-in-law. (*He pulls Davenport* *across him)*

Davenport His big brother-in-law.

Vic manages a wave

Slater (*to Davenport*) It's marvellous the way the family have rallied round so quickly.

Henry You have to, don't you? (*To Davenport*) Weren't you hoping to catch the overnight train to Manchester, Archie?

Davenport (*broadly*) Well, I was, yes—but I'm beginning to think maybe I should stay. (*He hands Henry the suitcase*)

Henry No, there's no need. (*To Vic*) Is there, Percy?

Vic None that I can think of! No, there's no need, Freddy.

Davenport Oh! Freddy? (*He beams at Henry*)

Henry (*to Davenport*) You have to catch your train, Archie. And then the next time I see you, I'll *reimburse* you the cost of the ticket and all your expenses.

Davenport I don't think I'm in any rush, actually—*Freddy.*

Henry Yes, you *are*, Archie. You've got to get back on the road.

Davenport On the road?

Henry Selling whatever travelling salesmen are selling these days.

Davenport Oh! Yes! No, I've got the weekend off.

Slater Anyway, he probably wants to stay for the funeral.

Davenport smiles hugely

Henry Oh, my God! (*He moves* DL *and puts the suitcase down*)

Davenport (*brightly*) Oh, there's a *funeral*, is there?

Slater Didn't you know, sir?

Davenport Not the exact particulars, no!

Vic I expect Freddy had only got as far as him not looking too well.

Henry moves in and glares at Vic

Henry Yes, thanks, Percy, I had. (*To Davenport*) The sad fact is, Archie—Henry died.

Davenport (*with great mock concern*) Oh, no, Freddy!

Henry Yes, Archie.

Davenport (*to Vic*) Last time I saw him I thought he was looking a bit pale, Percy.

Vic No, he was drowned in the river, Archie.

Henry Percy! Spare Archie the details, please.

Davenport Oh no, give me the details, please.

Slater (*to Davenport*) I'm afraid your brother Henry has been found dead in the river at Putney. His arms and legs had been tied together and he'd been shot in the back of the head.

Davenport Henry always had suicidal tendencies, you know.

Slater (*to Davenport*) I regret to say it looks like murder, Mr Perkins. (*He puts his briefcase by the right side of the armchair*) I'm waiting for Mrs Perkins to accompany me to the mortuary as soon as she's had a cup of tea. (*He moves up towards the kitchen*)

Henry (*to Davenport*) Yes, well, now you clearly intend to stay for the funeral, Archie...

Davenport I wouldn't miss it for the world, Freddy.

Henry Yes. Well—(*to Vic*) Percy——

Vic (*rising*) I don't think I can manage the funeral, Freddy.

Henry You stay here, Percy! While I sort out Jean, Sergeant Slater and the mortuary—you accompany my brother Archie into the dining-room.

Vic Oo, I don't think that's a good idea.

Henry Yes! Discuss how much cash Archie might expect to get—from poor Henry's will.

Davenport Now, that's a *very* good idea. (*He opens the dining-room door*)

Henry Yes, and I'll send you in a quick cup of tea.

Slater I hope it's quicker than the one I've had.

Davenport (*to Vic*) Come on, Percy. You can fill in the blank spots for me.

Davenport exits into the dining-room and sits on one of the chairs

Henry There's no need to fill in *all* the blank spots, Percy.

Vic I don't know the answer to *any* of the blank spots.

Henry pushes a bewildered Vic into the dining-room and closes the door

Henry (*calling in*) Just plead ignorance! (*He turns to Slater*) Now—where were we?

Slater Well, before the family gathering, I was waiting for Mrs Perkins to pull herself together—and a cup of tea.

Jean, in a highly emotional and inebriated state, comes in from the kitchen, followed by Betty. Jean is carrying a mug of milk and a half full bottle of cooking sherry

Jean I don't care, I'm going to bed.
Betty Jean...!
Slater (*surprised*) Going to bed?
Jean (*to Henry*) In the spare room!
Henry You can't go to bed, you're leaving! (*To Slater*) For the mortuary.
Slater She can't go to the mortuary dressed like that.
Jean I'm going to bed with a glass of milk and a half a dozen aspirins. (*To Henry*) In the spare room.
Betty She just can't bear to be in her own bed without Henry.
Jean I couldn't care less about Henry!

Jean runs upstairs

Slater reacts to Jean's remark

Slater That's a bit callous, I must say.
Betty (*to Slater*) She obviously can't forgive Henry for suddenly dying like this—on his birthday, as well.

Betty hurries upstairs

Slater Mr Perkins didn't die on his birthday, did he?
Henry (*sadly*) Yes. We never thought Henry would snuff it before the candles.

The telephone rings. Henry looks at it and back to Slater. He smiles at Slater and shrugs

Slater Aren't you going to answer it?
Henry It's a wrong number.
Slater How do you know?
Henry I can tell by the ring.

Slater picks the receiver up. Henry looks worried

Slater (*into the phone*) Hello? ... What? ... Brerfcurse? Wrong number.

(*He puts the phone down. To Henry*) You were right! You should get
your number changed.

Henry That's a very good idea, Sergeant. Look, why don't you make the
tea while I go and see to Mrs Perkins. (*He pushes Slater* R *and opens the
kitchen door*)

Slater Well, OK. But I've got to get her to the mortuary.

Henry (*sadly*) We're dealing with human emotions here, Sergeant.

Slater Yes, I understand that. Maybe I should get a doctor for Mrs
Perkins?

Henry (*stopping him*) God, no, we haven't got room for anyone else in
here!

Henry pushes Slater into the kitchen

*He then grabs his briefcase from the right end of the settee and starts to
hurry up the stairs*

(*Calling upstairs*) Come on, Jean, we're off!

A worried Vic appears from the dining-room

Vic Henry!

Henry Ah! (*He trips up the stairs. He rises, leaving his briefcase on the
bottom stair*)

Vic Henry!

Henry Henry is in the mortuary in Putney!

Vic Henry's bloody lucky I can tell you!

Henry glares at Vic

Henry Well, come on, what's the matter?

Vic I'm making a right cock-up in there with Sergeant Davenport.

Henry I thought you were pleading ignorance!

Vic So far my pleading ignorance has cost you another twenty thousand
pounds.

Henry Twenty thousand?!

Vic First of all he wants ten thousand pounds for not spilling the beans
about Henry, Percy, Freddy and Archie.

Henry God! And what's the other ten thousand for?

Vic That's five thousand apiece for not spilling the beans about our hanky panky under the blanket.

Henry That's outrageous! I'm not paying *your* five thousand for a start!

Henry strides into the dining-room

Vic Henry!

Betty hurries downstairs in a state

Betty Vic, Jean's locked herself in the loo.

Vic Good!

Betty She's turned the radio on full blast and I can't make myself heard.

Vic Sounds like utter bliss!

Vic exits into the dining-room

Betty Vic! (*She hurries to the dining-room door and listens. She then kneels down and looks through the keyhole*)

Slater comes out of the kitchen with a steaming teapot. He stops on seeing Betty looking through the keyhole. He coughs gently

Betty hesitates and then turns round

Just checking on my Percy—I can't quite see what he's doing in there with Freddy and Archie.

Slater looks blank

Slater I'll get the cups.

Slater exits to the kitchen still carrying the teapot

Henry storms out of the dining-room, followed by Vic, who closes the door

Henry Why the hell didn't you leave the talking to me!

Betty What's happened?

Henry Your husband only blurts out how much was in Mr Nasty's briefcase. (*He points to the dining-room*) He was happy to settle for an extra twenty thousand pounds.

Vic I'm sorry.

Henry You start saying it's easier to deal in percentages and it's cost me ten percent of seven hundred and thirty-five thousand! (*He collects his briefcase and sits on the right end of the settee*)

Vic But he did agree that was all inclusive. The original twenty-five, your sudden death and our hanky panky under the blanket. (*He sits in the centre of the settee*)

Betty Your hanky panky under the...?

Henry Never mind! Where's Jean? (*He opens his briefcase*)

Betty She's locked in the loo listening to Classic FM. (*She sits on the left end of the settee*)

Henry Ask a silly question! (*He now has the bundle of money in his hand*) Right, first let's pay off Sergeant Davenport.

Slater enters from the kitchen, carrying the teapot

Slater Right, now!

Henry slams the lid of the briefcase shut and throws the blanket over the three of them with their hands under the blanket and the blanket up to their necks. Slater walks down and they all smile at him. He is as bemused as always. Under the blanket, Henry locks the briefcase

Vic What can we do for you, Sergeant?

Slater (*flatly*) I was wondering—how many cups?

Betty What?

Slater Who's having tea?

Betty The whole family, except Mrs Perkins.

Slater Oh. And what about Archie?

Henry No, he's drinking nothing but champagne from now on. (*He glares at Vic and slides from under the blanket, surreptitiously passing the briefcase to Vic*) It's just the three of us. You're being most kind. (*He indicates for Slater to return to the kitchen*)

Slater (*not moving*) Has Mrs Perkins' condition not improved, then?

Henry No.

Betty No, I'm afraid not...

Slater I've been thinking.

Henry No, you don't want to do that. (*He indicates for him to go into the kitchen*)

Slater Well, it doesn't actually have to be Mrs Perkins.

Henry What doesn't?

Slater To identify the body. It's not legally necessary. If she's not physically or emotionally up to it and with all that alcohol——

Henry You mean—somebody else could identify Henry?

Slater Any relative would be officially acceptable. *You* could do it.

Henry Me? Oh, no, I couldn't identify Mr Perkins.

Slater Well, some other close relative, then.

After a brief moment, Henry and Betty smile and look to Vic. Vic realizes the situation

Vic Oh, no! Not me!

Slater It's not unusual for one of the gentlemen in a bereaved family to volunteer for the job.

Vic I never volunteer on principle.

Betty It's not a bad idea, Percy.

Henry It's a *very good* idea, Percy.

Vic (*mortified*) Identify that body as Henry Perkins?

Henry Please, Percy!

Vic I've just remembered, I can't.

Betty Why not?

Vic We're leaving for Australia in five minutes.

Betty We'll take the next flight.

Henry And you'd be well paid, Percy.

Slater (*surprised*) Paid? There's no payment involved in this, Mr Perkins.

Henry There might be. For him. For Percy. Expenses.

Slater He's only got to go to Putney.

Henry But he's come all the way from Australia, hasn't he? Look, you let the family sort this out privately and by the time you've made the tea we will have resolved the situation. (*He opens the kitchen door*)

Slater I've already made the tea.

Henry That'll be cold by now, you make it again.

Henry pushes Slater in the kitchen and slams the door

Please, Vic! Go to the mortuary.

Vic Identify that body as Henry Perkins? Definitely not!

Betty You're being very unhelpful, Vic.

Vic (*pointing at Henry*) He had no right to involve us in his nefarious activities.

Henry pulls the blanket from Vic, takes the briefcase and sits on the right end of the settee

Henry And I'm prepared to pay you cash.

Vic It's not a question of—how much?

Henry Ten thousand.

Vic Thirty.

Henry Twenty.

Vic Twenty-five.

Henry Done.

They shake hands

It's amazing the way it goes, isn't it?

Betty I'm very surprised at you, Vic. First the car, now this. You don't take money for helping a friend.

Vic He's not a friend, he's family!

Henry glares at Vic

Henry Betty, quick! Go and get Jean down here fast. (*He pushes Betty towards the stairs*)

Betty I told you, she's locked herself in the loo.

Henry Well, break the door down!

Betty Break the door?! Cor, this is living!

Betty hurries upstairs

Henry (*to Vic*) Right. Come on, give me the keys to your car.

Vic You give me the money first.

Henry Blimey, you're a tough negotiator, Vic. (*He opens the briefcase and starts to count out the money*)

Vic It's a cruel world, Henry. That's twenty-five thousand for identifying the body plus seven and a half thousand for the car.

Henry I know that!
Vic That adds up to thirty-two and a half thousand.
Henry I know that too!

Davenport enters from the dining-room

Davenport Mr Perkins!
Henry ⎫
Vic ⎭ *(together)* Ahh!

Henry and Vic automatically pull the blanket to their necks

Henry *(realizing)* Oh, it's you!
Davenport I'm still waiting.
Henry *(glaring at Vic)* Something popped up.
Davenport Under the blanket, was that?
Henry ⎫
Vic ⎭ *(together)* No!

They throw the blanket down

Davenport *(chuckling)* No, your secret's safe with me—providing, of
    course, I receive that extra "charitable donation" we'd agreed upon.
Henry All right, all right.

*Davenport sits on the left end of the settee next to Vic as Henry counts the
money*

Davenport Ten per cent I think you said, Mr Perkins.
Henry I didn't say it, *he* said it. (*He glares at Vic as he hands the money
    across Vic to Davenport*) There! That's less the twenty-five thousand
    you've already had.
Davenport Quite right. (*He takes the money*) All in a good cause.
Henry *(to Vic)* And there's yours. Thirty-two and a half thousand. (*He
    holds out the money*)
Davenport *(to Vic)* You're not diddling him as well, are you?
Vic I'm being paid for services rendered.

Davenport grins and Henry nearly dies

Davenport You cheeky thing, Percy! (*He chuckles*)

Slater enters from the kitchen

Slater Mr Perkins, where do you keep your cups and...?

Henry quickly slams the lid of the briefcase and pulls the blanket up to his, Vic's and Davenport's necks. Slater, bemused, walks down watching them as, under the blanket, they struggle with the bundles of money. Finally, the thrashing about ceases. Henry and Vic smile weakly. Under the blanket, Henry locks the briefcase. Davenport smiles happily at Slater who is looking agog

Davenport (*lightly*) He's caught the three of us at it now.

Henry and Vic close their eyes in anguish

(*To Vic*) We like to keep it in the family, don't we, Percy?

Vic buries his head

Henry Thank you, Archie!
Davenport He's a Police Officer, Freddy. He's seen it all before, haven't you, Sergeant?

Slater just shakes his head

Slater (*firmly*) I actually came in to ask where Mrs Perkins keeps her cups and saucers.
Henry (*flatly*) In the cupboard over the sink.
Slater You sure you all want a cup of tea?
Davenport Not half, thirsty work this.
Henry Thank you, Archie!
Slater Look. I think we'd better forget the tea, shall we? (*He turns and collects his briefcase from R of the armchair*)

Henry slides out from under the blanket, surreptitiously placing his briefcase on the floor at the right end of the settee

Henry (*moving to Slater*) That's a very good idea, Sergeant. Especially as Percy is now ready to accompany you to the mortuary. (*He moves* L *and opens the front door*)

Slater (*to Vic*) Oh, you've decided to accept that obligation, have you?

Vic (*weakly*) Yes.

Slater Well, thank heavens for that. Right, let's get going then, Mr Brown.

Vic Could you just give me five minutes to get ready?

Slater Five minutes?

Davenport (*suppressing a grin*) Yes, he's got his hands full at the moment.

Slater looks to heaven

Vic Thank you, Archie!

Slater marches to the door

Slater (*to Vic*) I'll wait for you in the car, Mr Brown. (*Pointedly*) You can sit in the back.

Slater exits through the front door

Vic (*to Davenport*) You rotten devil!

Davenport (*laughing*) Only a bit of fun, Percy. (*He rises. To Henry*) Well, it's been a real pleasure doing business with you, Mr Perkins. (*He throws his bundle of money in the air and catches it*)

Henry Thank you!

Davenport So—Percy here was telling me you're leaving for Barcelona.

Henry Percy should keep his trap shut.

Davenport Like I said, your secret's safe with me. You'll like Spain, though. You'll be really at home there.

Henry Full of Englishmen, you mean?

Davenport No. Full of crooks.

Davenport grins and exits through the front door

Vic starts to count his money

Henry Well, crooks or no crooks, you're dealing with Sergeant Slater, I've paid off Sergeant Davenport, and Barcelona, here I come. What are you doing, Vic?

Vic Ssh. I'm checking you haven't short changed me.

*Jean, still quite tipsy and still wearing her dressing-gown, enters on to
the stairs, being frogmarched by Betty. Betty is also carrying Jean's
clothes—bra, pants, slip and dress*

Jean Vic, I want you to know that your wife has broken our bathroom door
down and assaulted my person!
Betty Be quiet, you're going to Barcelona with Henry.
Jean I can't even *say* Barlecona.
Betty And he's giving you a thousand pounds a week for housekeeping,
aren't you, Henry?
Henry A thousand!
Jean I wouldn't go, even if you offered me five hundred!
Betty And you can get dressed in Vic's car on the way. (*She thrusts the
clothes on to Jean*)
Jean I'm not getting—— (*She stops*) Vic's car?
Betty It might not look much, but your husband's paid him seven and a
half thousand for it.
Henry (*pointedly, to Vic*) And a further twenty-five thousand to go to the
mortuary. (*He gets his raincoat from the armchair and puts it on*)
Jean (*looking at Vic; confused*) Vic's going to the mortuary?
Betty Yes!

Vic looks up from counting the money

Vic That's what happens when you leave the room for five minutes.

Henry gets Jean's coat from the cupboard

Jean Lovely. Vic's going to the mortuary, I'm going to bed and Henry's
going to Barlecona. (*She throws the clothes over her shoulder*)
Henry (*to Jean*) Put your coat on! (*He throws the coat at Jean and goes
for his briefcase*)
Jean Don't need a coat in bed. (*She throws the coat over her shoulder*)

Betty collects the clothes and coat

Betty You're going with Henry! (*She thrusts the clothes on to Jean*)

Jean Why won't anybody listen?! I'm not spending the rest of my life as Mrs Shufflebottom in Barlecona. (*She throws her clothes and coat over her shoulder*)

Henry puts his briefcase by the right side of the armchair

Henry Jean, we'll discuss this on the plane, you're a little bit sloshed.
Jean Henry, there's nothing to discuss and I'm a lot sloshed.
Vic Henry!
Henry What?!
Vic (*holding up the money*) It's all here.
Henry Good!
Vic Here are the car keys. (*He hands Henry the keys*)
Henry (*grabbing them*) Thank you!
Betty Jean, he's your husband. Better or worse, richer or poorer.
Jean Insanity wasn't on the list, was it?
Henry You'll push me too far, Jean. I'll go by myself. I will! I'll go by myself. On the plane. By myself to Barcelona.
Jean I hope you have a good flight, Henry.
Henry (*looking to Betty for moral support*) Oh, Betty!
Betty Jean, for heaven's sake, Henry needs looking after.
Jean Then he'll have to find some other Mrs Shufflebottom to look after him, won't he?

Betty goes to collect the clothes

Henry Don't think I couldn't. Cor! There must be a thousand women who'd jump at the chance of sharing my new life in Barcelona.
Jean Name one!
Henry More than a thousand.
Jean Come on. Name me one woman.
Betty (*putting her hand up*) Betty Johnson!

They all look at Betty. Vic rises

Well, I would. I mean, I think it sounds brilliant. I'd go like a shot.
Jean You what?!
Betty Well, if you don't fancy it—and if Henry would take me.
Jean Betty!

Vic There *is* something wrong with my hearing!

Jean I have never heard of anything so immoral! Henry, tell her where she gets off!

Henry You get off in Barcelona, Betty.

Jean Just a minute, just a minute! What about me?

Henry You won't go, will you?

Betty You can still change your mind, you know, Jean.

Jean Oh no, I don't want to spoil anyone's fun!

Betty You understand, don't you, Vic?

Vic shakes his head

Henry Wait a minute! Jean can't stay here. Mr Big will have this place surrounded by tomorrow.

Betty There's only one thing for it, then.

Henry What's that?

Betty Jean will have to go and live with Vic.

Jean With Vic?

Vic Hang on!

Betty In Clapham.

Vic Hang on, hang on!

Betty She'll be safe with Vic.

Vic Hang on, hang on, hang on!

Henry Betty, you're an absolute brick!

Vic Hang on, hang on, hang on, hang on!

Jean Just a minute!

Henry If you insist on staying, it'll stop me worrying if I know you're with Vic in Clapham. (*He turns to Vic*) Thanks Vic. (*He shakes Vic's hand*)

Vic Don't mention it.

Henry picks up his briefcase

Henry Right. We'd all better get going, then. Well, I'll say goodbye, then, Jean.

Jean (*nodding blankly*) Yes.

Henry I won't be able to make any contact with you.

Jean No.

For a brief second Henry is at a loss

Henry Oh! Betty, do you have an up-to-date passport?

Betty Oh, it's at home.

Henry We'll pick it up on the way to the airport. (*He collects the suitcase*)

Betty God, this is exciting, isn't it, Vic?

Vic Fantastic! (*He moves to Henry*) Well, you look after my wife, Henry.

Henry And you look after mine, Vic. Now, go on, Sergeant Slater's waiting out there to take you to the mortuary. (*To Jean*) Jean, we'll drop you off at Betty's place when we pick up her passport.

Jean We're leaving the house in a bit of a mess, Henry.

Betty You can tidy mine up, it's disgusting.

Bill comes in through the front door

Bill OK, are we ready?

They all look suitably surprised

Henry Ah, Ben!

All Bill!!

Henry Bill! We were told you'd gone off in a huff.

Bill Yes, well, I realized that wasn't very professional.

Henry Quite right.

Bill Beside, I wouldn't have got the fare paid, would I? Now! I'm taking Mr and Mrs Brown in my taxi to London Airport, right?

Henry No, Mr and Mrs Brown have gone by the board.

Bill Gone by what?

Henry Never mind. *I'm* going to London Airport.

Bill But I thought you said you weren't!

Henry Never mind!

Bill All right, let's get moving, then.

Henry No, I'm going in Mr Johnson's car. You can take Mrs Perkins now you're here.

Bill To London Airport?

Henry No, to Mrs Johnson's house in Clapham Common.

Bill (*surprised*) You're going to the Airport—and I'm taking you (*he moves to Jean*) to Clapham Common?

Jean That's where I'm living now.

Bill (*to Betty*) So you and Mrs Perkins are coming with me to Clapham.

Betty No. Mrs Perkins is going to Clapham. I'm going to Barcelona.

Bill Barcelona?!

Henry Yes!

Bill (*to Vic*) So you and your wife are going to *Barcelona* now, are you?

Vic No, she's going to Barcelona. I'm going to the mortuary with a policeman.

Bill assimilates this

Bill The mortuary with a...?

Henry *I'm* going to Barcelona!

Bill (*surprised*) With this fellow's wife? (*He points to Betty*)

Henry That's right! (*He thrusts the suitcase at Bill. To Betty*) Come on!

Bill Hold it! (*To Vic*) He's taking your wife to Barcelona?

Vic Yes!

Bill (*to Jean*) And you're going to live with him in Clapham? (*He points to Vic*)

Jean Yes!

Bill I don't know how me and the wife missed out on this sexual revolution.

Henry Wait outside!

Bill exits with the suitcase

Now come on, all of us. We've got to get going.

Jean returns to attempting to find her missing coat sleeve

Jean, put your coat on properly.

Jean I can't, somebody's stolen one of my sleeves.

Bill pops his head round the front door

Bill Is the suitcase going to Clapham Common or London Airport?

Henry It doesn't matter.

Bill If course it does, one's west, the other's south.

Henry Do as you're told!

Henry pushes Bill out

Bill (*as he is pushed*) I'm getting road rage!

Henry Just wait outside.

Bill exits

Vic, go to the mortuary! (*He pulls Vic across him*)

Vic I want to make sure there's no more change of plans. The rate we're going, I'll come home and find *you* waiting for me in bed. (*He sits in the armchair*)

Jean (*yawning*) Oh, lovely! Bed! Where do you keep your nighties, Betty?

Betty I don't wear nighties.

Henry (*beaming*) Don't you?

Vic (*rising; to Henry*) Hey!

Henry Sorry, Vic!

Betty Will you get going, Vic? (*She turns to Henry*) This is it, then. (*She offers her arm to Henry*)

Henry OK! (*Suddenly*) Oh, my God!

Betty What now?!

Henry No, this is serious.

Betty What is it?!

Henry Pussy!

Vic Pussy?

Henry (*to Vic*) Our ginger cat.

Jean I'd completely forgotten about Pussy!

Betty Never mind the cat, let's go.

Henry No, hang on. One of us has got to have Pussy.

Betty You'll get enough pussy in Barcelona, now come on!

Vic (*remonstrating*) Betty!

Henry No, hang on. (*To Jean*) Where *is* she?

Jean I haven't seen her all evening. I suppose Vic and I could come back tomorrow and look for her.

Henry Mr Big will have the place surrounded by then.

Vic Oh, my God, Mr Big! (*He sits fearfully in the armchair*)

Henry (*to Jean*) I bet you left the cat flap open.

Vic He wouldn't come through the cat flap, would he?

Henry Vic! (*He angrily puts his briefcase down at the right side of the armchair*)

Jean Good idea! A little cat nap. (*She sits and curls up on the settee*)

Henry Oh, no!

Betty (*trying to lift Jean*) You're going to bed at our place!

Slater comes in from the front door. He is angry and still holding his briefcase

Slater Right!

Henry, startled, sits on Vic's lap and Betty falls across Jean. Slater strides in to the middle of the room and bangs his briefcase down on the left side of the settee. He then sees the two couples. Vic has his arms around Henry's waist and the ladies appear to be locked in an embrace. He is shocked

(*Finally*) Mr Brown!
Henry (*to Vic*) That's you!
Vic Oh. Yes?
Slater I believe I said five minutes!
Vic And you said it very nicely.
Henry You did indeed, Sergeant. Come on, Percy, we've had enough hanky panky for one evening. (*He rises*) And we've all said our fond farewells, haven't we?

The ladies break their embrace. Vic rises

Vic (*hopelessly*) Why not? The mortuary's as good a place as anywhere else. (*He laughs*) Life's funny, isn't it? One minute you're bowling merrily along, the sun is shining, the birds are singing—all of a sudden, wham! No Pussy!

Vic exits

Slater looks totally bemused, picks up what he thinks is his briefcase (in fact it is the one with the money) from the right side of the armchair and exits

The others don't realize that Slater has taken the wrong briefcase

Betty Ah, that was quite poetic coming from Vic.
Henry Never mind Vic. Let's get Jean into the taxi, then we've got forty-five minutes before the check in.
Betty Ups-a-daisy!

Jean (*calling foolishly*) Puss, Puss, Puss, Puss, Pussy!
Henry Don't worry about Pussy. The neighbours will look after her.
Jean You're sure?
Henry Positive. They're always feeding her, anyway.
Jean No, I couldn't eat a thing, honestly.

They now have Jean upright, but with her coat on back to front. The telephone rings. Betty and Henry look to it and then back at each other

Bill enters from the front door

Bill Excuse me!
Henry ⎱ (*together*) Ahhh!
Betty ⎰

They drop Jean, who flops in a heap on the settee

Bill It's only that I've been waiting.
Henry Well, carry on waiting.

They all look at the phone, which is still ringing

Bill (*helpfully*) Telephone's ringing.
Henry We know that. (*He delicately picks up the receiver. Into the phone; in a broad Indian accent*) Taj Mahal, Indian take-away! ... What? I'm not understanding. We do Indian take-away, Vindaloo, Chippatti, Poppadom, Bhajee. We do Adelaide Bhajee, Percy Bhajee—we do Archie Bhajee... No, I am not understanding. Thank you for calling. Bye-bye. (*He replaces the receiver and looks at a bemused Bill. To Bill, in an Indian accent*) Well, come on, what are you wanting? (*He realizes*) Well, come on, what is it?
Bill Is Mrs Perkins ready yet?
Henry Very nearly.
Bill It's only that as Mr Johnson is about to depart, I was hoping the whole caravan was on the move.
Betty (*to Bill*) Mrs Perkins is coming now.
Henry Yes.

Bill looks at Jean who is still in a heap on the settee

Bill Is that Mrs Perkins?
Henry Yes. She's a little bit tipsy.
Bill She's totally plastered!
Henry We know that.
Bill She'd better not be sick in my taxi.
Betty Could you just wait outside and we'll see to Mrs Perkins.
Henry Yes.
Bill Right. By the way, I decided on Clapham Common for the suitcase.
Henry Lovely!

Bill crosses to Betty

Bill (*to Betty*) She is still going to Clapham Common, isn't she?
Henry Yes!
Bill Just checking!
Betty 344 Clapham Road.
Bill (*to Betty*) And that's your place?
Henry Yes!
Bill Just checking. (*To Betty*) And you're still going with him (*he points to Henry*) to Barcelona?
Henry (*to Bill*) That's nothing to do with you! (*He pulls Bill across him*)
Betty (*to Henry*) But we're stopping in Clapham on the way to London Airport.
Bill Clapham isn't actually on the way to London Airport.
Henry We're having a little diversion.
Bill Is that what they call it now?
Henry Get back in your cab!

Henry pushes Bill out

Betty Now, come on, Henry!
Henry Right!

They lift Jean. Jean surveys her back-to-front coat

Jean Am I coming or going?
Betty You're going!
Henry Oh! Wait a minute!
Betty You haven't got a dog as well as a cat, have you?
Henry No, I've suddenly realized.

Jean What?
Henry Under the circumstances——
Betty What?!
Henry We ought to split the cash.
Betty Split it?
Henry Between us. (*To Betty*) You and me. Jean and Vic. Now—where's my briefcase? (*He sees the briefcase left behind by Slater*) Ah! Fifty-fifty. Half each. (*He picks up the briefcase*)
Jean Henry! That's very generous of you.
Betty (*to Jean*) I thought you didn't want any of his ill-gotten gains?
Jean That was when he was taking me, now he's taking you. (*She sits in the armchair*)
Henry It's only fair, Betty. (*He sits on the L arm of the chair and goes to open the briefcase*)
Betty Well, be quick, for goodness sake.

The phone rings. Betty and Henry freeze

Henry Leave it.
Betty It might be Mr Big again.
Henry All the more reason to leave it. Come on.

They pick Jean up

   Bill enters through the front door

Bill Excuse me...!
All (*together; jumping*) Ahhhh!

They drop Jean into the armchair. She slips to the floor

Bill I don't know if anybody cares——
Henry Ssh!

They pick Jean up

Bill —but the meter now reads thirty-seven pounds fifty——
Henry |
            | (*together*) Ssh!
Betty |

They drop Jean into the armchair

Bill —and so far the taxi hasn't moved a bloody inch!
Betty
Henry } (*together*) Ssh!
Jean

They pick Jean up as Bill picks up the phone

Bill (*into the phone*) Hello?
Henry } (*together*) No!
Betty

Betty lets go of Jean. Jean slumps on to Henry

Bill (*into the phone*) No, there's nobody called Brerfcurse here.
Henry No! (*He drops Jean into the armchair*)

Jean slips to the floor

Bill (*into the phone*) No, this is Perkins, 42 Elgar Avenue, Fulham——
Henry } (*together*) No!
Betty

Henry grabs the receiver and bangs it down

Bill All I said was "42 Elgar Avenue".
Henry (*mortified*) You've given our address to Mr Big!
Bill Who's Mr Big?
Jean (*sitting up; half asleep*) Mr Brerfcurse.
Bill Who's Mr Brerfcurse?

Henry puts the briefcase on the coffee table

Henry Betty! Quick, get in the car. (*He gives her the keys*) Start the
   engine. (*To Jean*) You, get in the taxi.

Betty starts to pull Jean up

Bill Thank God for that!

Henry No, don't get in the taxi.

Bill For crying out loud!

Henry We've still got to halve the "you know what". (*He flicks his fingers across Bill, pointing at his briefcase*)

Bill smacks Henry's hand

Bill Halve the "you know what"?!

Henry Sssh!

Betty We'll never get to Barcelona at this rate.

Bill By the way, when did you elbow Sydney for Barcelona?

Henry Ssh!

Betty Jean! You come with us in the car. (*To Henry*) We'll sort out the finances on the way to Clapham. (*She pulls Jean to her*)

Henry Good thinking. (*To Bill*) We don't need the taxi at all.

Bill (*exasperated*) I don't believe it.

Henry Betty, get Jean in the car. (*He goes to his briefcase* DR)

Bill Hey, hey, hey!

Henry What now?

Bill Thirty-seven pounds fifty.

Henry God!

Bill Plus tip.

Henry It'll have to be a fifty pound note, that's all I've got.

Bill Smashing. I don't carry any change.

Henry sits on the settee and puts the briefcase on the coffee table

Henry (*to Bill; opening the briefcase*) If we miss our plane it'll be all thanks—— (*He has opened the briefcase. He stops and stares inside. For a moment he is silent. Suddenly*) Ahhhhh! (*He bangs the lid shut*)

Bill (*covering his ears*) God Almighty!

Jean What's all the noise about, Henry?

Henry hesitates, then opens the briefcase again

Henry Ahhhh! (*He bangs the lid shut*)

Bill (*covering his ears*) God Almighty!

Betty For heaven's sake, Henry, what is it?

Henry opens the lid. Bill, preparing for a scream, covers his ears

Henry Anybody fancy a cheese and chutney sandwich? (*He takes out the sandwich*)

Jean (*agog*) That's your briefcase!

Betty Henry!

Bill I wouldn't mind a cheese and chutney sandwich. (*He takes the sandwich and has a bite*)

Betty What's happened, for God's sake?

Henry I'll tell you what's happened. Your husband has gone off with Sergeant Slater, who is clutching a briefcase containing seven hundred and thirty-five thousand pounds.

Bill chokes on his mouthful of sandwich

Bill (*spluttering*) Seven hundred and thirty-five...

Henry shuts the briefcase and locks it

Henry That's it! We've had it! We've lost the lot!

Jean (*comfortingly*) Henry, I'm so sorry.

Henry puts the briefcase down by the coffee table

Henry (*rising*) I had it all. Barcelona! Bali! Bloody wife swapping!

Bill considers this for a moment

Bill Is that through Thomas Cook's?

Henry glares at Bill

Henry No, that's it! Back to the office on Monday!

Jean I don't know why, but I suddenly feel very sober.

Betty (*suddenly*) Henry! What'll you say to Mr Big?

Henry (*realizing*) Oh, my God! Mr Big!

Bill Is Mr Big going to give me my thirty-seven pounds fifty?

Henry No, he's not!

Vic comes through the front door

Vic Henry!

There is a momentary pause

Henry (*delighted*) Vic!
Vic Henry——
Henry Vic! (*He hugs Vic*) You haven't gone! Where's Sergeant Slater?
Vic Outside.
Betty (*to Vic*) We thought you'd left for the mortuary!
Vic You're not going to believe this.
Betty To identify a dead body.
Vic I just have. We've run over their cat.

Jean screams and rushes out of the front door

Betty Jean!

Betty hurries out after Jean

Bill I'll give you a hand. (*He goes to move but turns to Vic*) Is it a lot
  squashed or just a little bit?
Henry Get out!
Bill I'll give 'em a hand.

Bill hurries out through the front door

Vic I'm sorry, Henry.
Henry It's all right, Vic!
Vic It ran straight under the Sergeant's car.
Henry Could happen to anyone. Where's the briefcase?
Vic I'm sure it was painless—(*he stops*)—briefcase?
Henry With the money!

Vic points to the briefcase by the coffee table

Vic Isn't that it?
Henry That's mine.
Vic (*confused*) Well, if that's yours… (*He realizes*) That's yours? You
  mean "cheese and chutney" yours?
Henry Sergeant Slater must have picked up the other one by mistake.
Vic Jeeze!
Henry Where is he?

Vic Digging a hole for the cat.

Henry Somehow we've got to swap them back. (*He goes to pick up the "cheese and chutney" briefcase*)

Slater enters from the front door, carrying the "money" briefcase

Slater Good news!

Henry and Vic turn

It's all right!

Henry (*relieved*) Sergeant Slater! (*He hurries over to Slater, eyeing Slater's briefcase*)

Slater She's only stunned.

Henry I beg your pardon?

Slater Mrs Perkins' cat. Dazed, that's all.

Henry Oh, that's wonderful! Isn't that wonderful, Percy?

Vic Yes, Freddy, it would have been tragic, Jean losing her husband and her pussy all in one go.

Slater So, let's get moving, Mr Brown.

Henry Do you know what, Sergeant? (*He pulls Slater across him to the centre of the room*)

Slater (*tersely*) What?

Henry We never had that cup of tea. (*He takes hold of Slater's briefcase and gently pulls it to himself*)

Slater doesn't let go. During the ensuing exchange, behind Slater's back, Henry indicates for Vic to pick up the other briefcase from DR. After a moment of hesitation, Vic does so. Vic tip-toes behind Slater and Henry to end up on the left side of Henry

Slater (*trying to control himself*) I don't want a cup of tea. (*He pulls the briefcase back*)

Henry doesn't let go

Henry You sit down, you haven't had a break all evening. (*He pulls the briefcase back*)

Slater (*more fiercely*) I don't want a break, Mr Perkins! I want to take my leave of 42 Elgar Avenue and go to the mortuary with Mr Brown! (*He pulls the briefcase*)

Henry (*pulling the briefcase*) But a cup of tea would——

Slater (*interrupting*) I waited an hour for a cup of tea—(*he pulls the briefcase back; through gritted teeth*) and I have been very patient with you——

Henry You certainly have. (*He pulls the briefcase*)

Slater —and the many members of your large family. (*He pulls the briefcase back*)

Henry And the many members will remember that. (*He pulls the briefcase*) Why don't you let me relieve you——

Slater I don't want to be relieved. (*He pulls the briefcase back*)

Henry Well, that's a relief. (*He pulls the briefcase, and this time it comes out of Slater's hand and ends up on the other side of Henry*)

In one deft movement, Vic, who has been standing on the other side of Henry with the "cheese and chutney" briefcase, exchanges the briefcases

Slater (*eyeball to eyeball with Henry*) Look! (*He grabs hold of what he assumes is his briefcase and pulls it firmly to him*) I am very aware of the distress that Mr Perkins' tragic death has caused——

Henry You have been most kind and sympathetic.

Slater —I must now insist on going to the mortuary with Mr Brown!

Henry (*politely*) You only had to ask. Mr Brown here is awaiting your pleasure. (*He pulls Vic across him to Slater and, at the same time, relieves Vic of the "money" briefcase. He walks behind them and puts his briefcase down by the left side of the coffee table*)

Slater (*forcefully*) Mr Brown! You are required to accompany me and make a formal identification of the body found in the river at Putney.

Vic After this anything will be a relief.

Henry (*delighted*) Off you go, Mr Brown! Sergeant Slater!

Jean comes in through the front door. She is now wearing her coat the right way round

Jean (*entering*) Thank goodness! Pussy's all right, Henry!

Henry (*calling up to heaven*) Did you hear that, Henry? Pussy's all right!

Vic looks up to heaven, so does Slater. Slater closes his eyes in anguish

Slater (*to Vic*) Let's go.

Slater storms out through the front door with the briefcase

Henry turns to Vic and hugs him

Henry You were brilliant, Vic! (*To Jean*) We've got the money back.
Jean I've been more worried about the cat.
Henry I'm halving it with you!
Vic Halving the cat?
Henry Vic! (*He picks up his briefcase*)
Jean Bill's looking after her at the moment. She's got a little bump, that's all.
Henry Great.
Jean You don't mind Pussy living with us, do you, Vic?
Vic I've given up minding about anything.
Henry Come on!
Jean (*to Vic*) I'll just get Pussy's cat box, Vic.
Vic Cat box, horsebox, chicken pox, please yourself.
Henry (*to Jean*) There's no time to get her cat box!
Jean And I'll bring some cat food.
Henry Mr Big has our address. He's on his way round here.
Vic (*horrified*) Mr Big has your address?
Henry Yes!

Vic sags at the knees

Vic When did that happen?
Henry Seven and three-quarter minutes ago. (*He shouts*) It doesn't matter when it happened, he's coming!
Vic Oh, my God!
Henry (*to Jean*) Forget the cat food.
Vic Yes, forget the cat food. I've got turkey, ice cream, lasagne——
Jean You haven't got flea powder.

Jean hurries out into the kitchen

Vic ⎫ (*together*) ⎧ Never mind the flea powder!
Henry ⎭   ⎩ Forget the flea powder!

Betty enters from the front door

Betty Henry!

Henry moves to Betty, showing her the briefcase

Henry Betty, we've got the money back!
Betty (*thrilled*) You clever fellow, Henry. (*She kisses him on the cheek*)
Vic Oy, you're not in Barcelona yet!
Henry (*to Betty*) I'll grab Jean. We're dropping her off at your place, remember?

Henry exits into the kitchen, still clutching the briefcase

Vic (*to Betty*) Well, if you'll excuse me, I've got an appointment at the mortuary.

Slater enters from the front door, carrying the "cheese and chutney" briefcase. He marches behind the armchair

Slater That's it!
Vic ⎱
Betty ⎰ (*together*) Ahh!

Slater bangs the briefcase down at the right side of the armchair

Slater That's bloody it! I've waited long enough for you, Mr Brown.
Vic I'm coming, I'm coming!
Slater So's Christmas!
Vic I'm ready, I'm ready.
Slater It's too late, mate. Where's your sister-in-law?
Vic (*confused*) Macclesfield, why?

Slater manages to control himself

Betty (*to Vic*) He means Jean.
Slater (*to Betty*) Yes, I mean Jean! Your mad sister! The mad widow! And the mad widow is going to identify her dead husband whether she likes it or not!

Vic No, *I* want to do that! I love dead bodies!

Before Slater can explode, Henry enters from the kitchen, still holding the briefcase

Henry Now Jean can't find the cat box.
Slater Never mind the cat box! (*To Betty*) Go and tell your sister she's coming with me to the mortuary!
Henry (*sweetly*) No, no. You've got it slightly wrong, Sergeant, Mr Brown is——
Slater Mr Brown is as nutty as everybody else in this family!
Henry That's as may be, but Mr Brown——
Slater Mrs Perkins is coming with me to Putney. And I don't care if the sight of the blood and her husband's horribly mutilated body give her screaming hysterics. (*To Betty*) Tell your sister if she's not in my car in one minute, I will arrest her!
Henry But Mrs Perkins is in no——
Slater (*cutting in; finally cracking*) You shut up! Shut up and shove off! And shove yourself right up your sheep in Sydney!

Slater, without thinking, snatches the briefcase from Henry and marches out of the front door

There is a pause during which Henry is too mortified to speak. Then, in a daze, he picks up the "cheese and chutney" briefcase

Henry (*blankly*) That's the second time he's done that.
Betty He seemed really pleasant when he first arrived.

Henry collapses on to the settee, putting the briefcase DR *of the settee*

Henry That's it! Sergeant Slater will find the cash, Mr Big will find us and we'll find ourselves with Mr Nasty in the mortuary.
Betty Henry, we've still got to clear off before Mr Big arrives.
Vic Oh God! Mr Big!
Henry Where can Jean and I go, we're broke!
Betty Vic! They'll both have to live with us in Clapham now.
Vic Hang on!

Betty hurries towards the kitchen

Betty I'll grab Jean. (*To Henry*) I'm really disappointed about you and me
and Barcelona, Henry.

Henry Me, too, Betty.

Betty (*to Vic*) Do you think we can have the same arrangement in
Clapham, Vic?

Vic No, we can't!

Betty opens the kitchen door

Betty Maybe once a year on your birthday, Henry.

Betty exits into the kitchen

Vic I don't know what's come over Betty.

Henry (*moving to the kitchen*) Betty! It's my birthday today!

Vic Henry! (*He stops Henry going into the kitchen*)

*Slater walks in the front door, looking totally dazed and still holding the
briefcase*

Henry (*delightedly*) Sergeant Slater!

Henry and Vic hurry to Slater

Slater (*flatly*) That taxi driver of yours has just reversed into my police car.

Henry (*happily relieved*) That's awful!

Slater (*flatly*) Which caused my police car to reverse into a pedestrian.

Henry That's terrible!

Vic Is it serious?

Slater (*suddenly shouting*) He's been hit by a motor vehicle, of course it's
serious!

Henry (*to Slater*) Would you like me to relieve you—— (*He puts his hand
out towards Slater's briefcase*)

Slater (*murderously*) If you come anywhere near me, so help me, you will
join your brother on that slab in the mortuary.

Henry Ah, point taken.

Slater An ambulance is on its way, so I'll have to stay until it's sorted out.

Henry is eyeing Slater's briefcase

Vic In the meantime, would it be all right if I left for Australia?

Slater You stay put!

Vic Of course.

Slater (*to Henry*) And you tell Mrs Perkins we're leaving for the mortuary the moment I've ascertained the extent of this fellow's injuries.

Henry (*eyeing Slater's briefcase*) I was wondering if I could——

Slater (*cutting in*) No, you couldn't. Where does Mrs Perkins keep her first aid kit?

Henry In the bathroom cabinet.

Slater Right! (*He hurries towards the stairs, still clutching his briefcase*)

Henry hurries up R *of the settee*

Henry (*calling*) Sergeant Slater!

Slater stops and turns to Henry

Slater What?

Henry Could I come upstairs and relieve you?

Slater No, you couldn't! (*He starts to march upstairs*)

Henry quickly picks up the other briefcase from DR *of the settee*

Henry (*yelling*) Sergeant—catch!

As Slater turns, Henry throws the briefcase in the air towards him. Slater drops his briefcase in order to catch the flying briefcase with two hands. Vic neatly catches the dropped briefcase.

Slater controls himself and exits

Henry and Vic give a "whoop" of delight. Henry rushes to Vic and embraces him and hugs him and kisses him on the cheek

Slater returns on to the stairs. He stops on seeing Henry kissing Vic. He walks down to behind Henry

Henry, still not seeing Slater, breaks the embrace

(*To Vic*) Oh, I love you!

To Slater's amazement, Henry cuddles Vic. He then holds Vic's face in his hands

(*To Vic*) Fantastic! That's twice you've done it to me! (*He hugs Vic again*)

Vic and Henry laugh delightedly. Slater puts his hand to his mouth and gives a cough to interrupt. They turn to Slater and their laugh fades

Slater (*flatly*) Would one of you two gentlemen be good enough to tell the taxi driver not to leave the premises. He may be needed as a material witness.

Henry Of course.

Slater And perhaps you could try to keep your hands off each other for five minutes.

Slater exits upstairs, still holding the briefcase

Vic Lovely. Two police forces are going to have me on their records now.

Henry (*laughing*) Vic! (*He takes the briefcase with the money*)

Jean enters from the kitchen, followed by Betty

Jean I'm so sorry, Henry.

Henry Why? What's happened now?

Jean Betty told me. Sergeant Slater's got your money.

Henry Oh, that's yesterday's news, isn't it, Vic?

Vic (*despondently*) Yes. Barcelona's on again.

Henry Yes! (*He shows the briefcase to Betty*)

Betty Is that the one with the cash?

Henry Certainly is.

Betty That's wonderful! (*To Jean*) Tell 'em. Jean.

Jean Well, I've been thinking——

Vic I wish people would stop doing that.

Jean ——and I've decided that I should go with you and Betty.

Henry is amazed

Henry (*pleased*) Jean!

Jean I think the brandy and the cooking sherry cleared my brain for me.

Henry That's terrific! Is this all right with you though, Betty? Jean coming with us?

Betty Of course it is. We'll share you.

Vic Hang on, hang on, hang on, hang on, hang on! Where does all this leave me?

Henry Facing a couple of charges of indecent behaviour.

Vic Just a second——

Henry (*laughing*) No! Now Jean's coming you'd better join us as well, Vic.

Vic What?!

Henry Make up the foursome!

Betty Of course, silly!

Jean Good old Vic!

Henry Now come on, Jean, if you're going to Barcelona, you'd better wear bra and pants. Change in the car.

Jean Oh, I'll have to see Bill before we go. Ask him to put Pussy into quarantine.

Henry Quarantine?

Jean Then, as soon as we've settled in, Bill can arrange to fly the cat over to us; then, when——

Henry (*cutting in*) Hang on, hang on. Bill doesn't work for nothing, you know. I'd better leave him a couple of thousand for expenses. (*He sits on the settee and puts the briefcase on his lap*)

Vic May I remind you that Mr Brerfcurse—alias Mr Big—will be paying us a visit any minute now!

Before Henry can open the briefcase, Slater enters down the stairs carrying a first aid box and the briefcase

Slater Right, let's sort this fellow out and get——

Vic, Jean and Betty sit quickly on the settee beside Henry, who throws the blanket over all of them and his briefcase. Jean and Henry are totally enveloped by the blanket. Slater stops, then walks down to the settee. In the rush, the bra and pants have been left outside the blanket. The bra and pants are "reeled in" by Jean from under the blanket, with Slater watching stony faced. Finally, Jean and Henry's heads appear from under the blanket. They smile at Slater

You lot really believe in fair shares for all, don't you?

Henry We were just having a family——
Slater (*cutting in*) I can see what the family was having, thank you!

Davenport enters through the front door

Davenport Evening all!
Jean
Betty } (*together*) Oh no!
Vic
Henry } (*together*) Oh God!

Davenport takes in the situation

Davenport Oh! (*To Slater*) Caught them at it again, have you?
Slater (*to Davenport*) I thought you were leaving for Manchester.
Henry Yes, we *all* thought that was the arrangement, Archie.
Davenport The train doesn't go till midnight, though, does it? Thought
   I'd pop back and cheer the family up a bit.
Vic We're very happy being miserable, thank you.
Davenport Lucky I did return, actually, there's been an accident outside
   your house.
Jean An accident?
Slater (*tersely*) That's all in hand, thank you, sir.
Davenport (*grinning*) Apparently you've run over a pedestrian.
Jean What!
Betty A pedestrian?!
Slater (*growling*) It wasn't my fault!
Davenport That's what they all say.
Betty Don't you think somebody should send for an ambulance?
Slater (*suddenly shouting*) I have sent for an ambulance! It's a pity you
   and your family don't help a bit instead of indulging in your Australian
   fetishes.

Slater storms out of the front door with the first aid box and the briefcase

Davenport You don't have to worry about the pedestrian. He's sitting on
   the pavement with his head in his hands.
Jean Dear oh dear.
Davenport It's OK, it's still on his shoulders.

Vic Now, can we please all go before Mr Big turns up?!
Henry Yes!
Davenport Oh, didn't I tell you? Mr Big's already here.

Henry, Jean, Vic and Betty look at each other, horrified. They all rise

Vic Here?
Henry Where?
Davenport Outside.
Jean |
Betty | (*together*) Outside?!
Davenport Yes, he's the injured pedestrian on the pavement.

They all react

Henry What?!
Davenport Sergeant Slater very kindly ran over Mr Big for you.
Jean How do you know it's him?
Davenport He's sitting there mumbling, "Brerfcurse, brerfcurse, brerfcurse".

They all look mortified

Henry Oh, my God!
Vic Does he look dangerous?
Davenport Not any more! He's got double vision, a sprained wrist and a broken ankle.
Betty Wonderful!
Davenport And a fractured jaw.
Jean That'll teach him for putting Mr Nasty in the river.
Henry That police car must have hit him pretty hard.
Davenport No, that only gave him the double vision. When I realized who he was *I* gave him the fractured jaw, the sprained wrist and the broken ankle.
Vic Blimey!
Henry (*delighted*) I reckon that's worth another five thousand, Sergeant. (*He moves to Davenport tapping his briefcase*)
Davenport I've been thinking about that, Henry. I mean, continually giving me these one-off settlements. Why not put me on the payroll permanently?

Henry On the payroll?

Davenport Yes. Take me to Barcelona with you.

They all look surprised

Henry Barcelona?

Davenport You need looking after, Henry. There's a lot of villains knocking about out there.

Vic (*pointedly referring to Davenport*) There's quite a few in here as well.

Jean It's not a bad idea, Henry. I mean, if people are going to put contracts on us.

Vic Hang on a second! (*To Davenport*) You're a serving Police Officer, aren't you?

Davenport I most certainly am.

Henry Well, what's your Superintendent going to say?

Davenport He'll be pleased to see me, he's been on the run in Spain for the last six months.

Henry (*laughing*) OK, you're on! Oh! Have you got a passport on you?

Davenport Don't be daft, I've got half a dozen.

Henry Right. We'll go the back way before Sergeant Slater returns. (*He shepherds everybody towards the kitchen*)

Betty Yes, please!

Henry Now, come on!

Jean Oh! (*To Henry*) You've got to give Bill some money for Pussy.

Davenport Money for...?

Vic Don't even ask!

Henry We'll send Bill the money from Barcelona.

Jean Oh! I'd better take this for the journey. (*She takes the whisky bottle from the sideboard*)

Henry (*taking the bottle from her*) I'll take that. You take this. (*He gives Jean the briefcase*)

Davenport Hey, can we all squeeze into Mr Brown's car?

Henry Definitely. And, just for the record, it's not Mr Brown's car, it's my car and it was very expensive.

Davenport (*to Vic*) Let's go, Mr Brown.

Vic (*to Davenport*) As we're going to be living together—the name's Johnson, not Brown.

Vic hurriedly exits into the kitchen

Davenport (*calling after him*) Got it, Percy!
Betty And it's Vic, not Percy.

Betty hurriedly exits into the kitchen

Davenport (*calling after her*) OK, Adelaide!
Jean It's not Adelaide, it's Betty. (*She moves to go into the kitchen*)
Davenport (*to Jean*) Excuse me! You and your husband are Jean and
  Henry, aren't you?
Jean Absolutely.

Jean exits into the kitchen

Davenport Thank God for that!
Henry Except to those who think we're Freddy and Genevieve, Archie.
Davenport And it's not Archie, it's Cecil.

Davenport exits

*Henry is about to follow, when Bill hurries in from the front door,
slamming the door behind him*

Bill Mr Perkins!
Henry Bill! You're supposed to be looking after our cat.
Bill Your cat's OK, it's in my taxi. It's Sergeant Slater I'm worried about.
Henry What's he up to now?
Bill He's not up to anything. He's been knocked down.
Henry By your taxi?
Bill No, by that pedestrian.
Henry What?!
Bill He hit him with his briefcase.
Henry Oh, my God!
Bill The Sergeant tried to take it from him and the fellow hit him with it,
  wallop. Out cold.
Henry Bloody hell!
Bill I reckon Mr Brerfcurse has got something illegal in his brerfcurse.
Henry How do you know about Mr Brerfcurse's brerfcurse?
Bill Come off it! I've heard enough in the last two hours to write a James
  Bond film.
Henry Well, where's Mr Brerfcurse now?

Bill Staggering up and down the road looking for number 42.

Henry Oh, my God!

Bill We'll go the back way, shall we?

Henry Good idea. (*He stops*) Hey! What do you mean "we"?

Bill I'm coming with you.

Henry To Barcelona?

Bill Why not? You've been paying everybody else to keep their trap shut.

Henry I've already got a security guard!

Bill You're dead lucky, you've got a gardener now as well.

Henry That makes six of us!

Bill Here, we might qualify for a group booking.

Vic enters from the kitchen

Vic We're waiting for you in the side street!

Henry All right, all right, I'm sorting out the terms of employment for the staff.

Vic Sorting out *what*?

Bill I've just been signed up as your gardener.

Vic I thought you were supposed to be looking after the cat.

Bill She'll be OK, I'll drop her off at my sister's and meet you at British Airways check-in.

Henry I hope you're as good at planning our garden.

Bill I'll give the old girl fifty quid for her trouble and you can add that to my first week's wages plus the thirty-seven pounds fifty plus tip.

Betty enters from the kitchen

Betty What's keeping everybody?!

Henry My money, by the look of things!

Vic (*to Betty*) Don't ask any questions. (*He refers to Bill*) His sister's looking after the cat for fifty quid and he's coming to Barcelona as our gardener.

Betty (*to Bill*) I thought you were a married man, Bill.

Bill I am. She'd never think of looking for me in Barcelona.

They all consider this

Betty Come on, then, the more the merrier.

Betty exits into the kitchen

Bill Right, my taxi's out the front, I'll have to go that way.

Henry You steer clear of Sergeant Slater!

Vic And Mr Brerfcurse!

Bill See you at London Airport. (*He sings*) "We're all going to sunny Spain."

Henry (*laughing*) We'll see you at the airport!

Henry pushes Bill out through the front door

Vic Now, come on!

Henry is bolting the front door

Henry All right, I'm just making sure!

The Passer-by enters from the kitchen. He is a very large man in a suit and a camel-hair overcoat. He looks very bedraggled and his expensive clothes are muddy and ripped from the accident. Right across his overcoat is the imprint of a black tyre mark. He also has a large bruise on his forehead and a black eye and is very dazed. He is hopping on one foot and carrying one wrist held out very limply. In his other hand he carries a briefcase

Henry and Vic turn to come face to face with the Passer-by

Henry
Vic } (*together; yelling*) Ahhh!

They grab each other in terror. The Passer-by looks from Henry to Vic. When he speaks, it is with some difficulty because of his fractured jaw

NB: Apart from the word "Brerfcurse", the Passer-by speaks only in Dutch. His dialogue is therefore given in Dutch, with phonetic pronunciation and English translation following in brackets

Passer-by (*finally; to Vic*) Brerfcurse!

Vic You'll have to speak clearer than that, sir.

Passer-by (*to Henry*) Brerfcurse! Geef me myn geld! (*Hayf mare mayn helt! / Give me my money*)

Henry I'm afraid we don't speak your lingo.

Passer-by (*to Vic*) Geef me myn geld! (*Hayf mare mayn helt! / Give me my money*)

Henry Hey, that sounds like Dutch.

Passer-by (*to Henry*) Geef me myn geld! Geef me myn geld! (*Hayf mare mayn helt! Hayf mare mayn helt! / Give me my money! Give me my money!*)

Vic And that sounds like double Dutch.

The Passer-by throws the briefcase on to the armchair and takes out a gun. He hops to Vic and brings the gun to Vic's head

I think I'm beginning to understand the lingo now. (*His knees give way and he sinks to the floor*)

Passer-by (*to Henry*) Ik tel tot vijf! (*Ik tel tot fayf! / I will count to five!*)

Henry I didn't quite get that.

Vic No, I'm going to get it! Give him the money!

Passer-by Een...! (*Ayn...! / One...!*)

Henry No, hang on a second! My wife's got the briefcase outside!

Passer-by Twee...! (*Tvay...! / Two...!*)

Henry We'll send for an interpreter!

Vic I don't *need* an interpreter! (*He closes his eyes*)

Passer-by Drie...! (*Dree...! / Three...!*)

Henry We'll do a deal, fifty-fifty!

Passer-by Vier...! (*Fear...! / Four...!*)

Vic We'll do a deal, take the lot!!

Passer-by Vijf...! (*Fayf...! / Five...!*)

Jean, still carrying the briefcase, comes in through the open kitchen door and bangs it closed

Jean Henry!

Vic (*screaming*) Ahh! (*He falls to the floor, yelling*)

The Passer-by turns and fires the gun, which hits the vase of flowers on the sideboard, smashing the vase and sending the flowers into the air. Henry drops to his knees and crawls to the armchair

Passer-by Brerfcurse! (*He points the gun at Vic's head again*)

Betty hurries through from the kitchen, slamming the door

Betty Vic!
Vic (*screaming*) *Ahhh!*

The Passer-by turns and fires the gun, which hits the radio, causing it to fly off the table DR *and music is heard*—Carmen. *They all look at the radio as the music gradually dies and grinds to a halt*

Betty (*nonchalantly*) Were you expecting visitors, Jean?
Jean (*nonchalantly*) No, I wasn't, Betty. Who do you think he is?
Betty Dunno. Looks like a rather effeminate tea-pot.
Henry Don't antagonize him, for God's sake!
Passer-by Brerfcurse!
Jean Oh! (*To Betty*) He wants the brerfcurse! (*She holds out her briefcase*)
Betty Let's give it to him, then, Jean! (*She takes the briefcase and offers it to the Passer-by*)

Before he can take it, Jean and Betty leap into the karate pose. Jean kicks the Passer-by's injured foot and Betty hits him in the midriff with the briefcase. He collapses to the ground

Passer-by Ahh!

Jean immediately treads on his sprained wrist

Ahhh! (*He throws the gun in the air*)

Bill enters from the kitchen

Bill What the heck is everybody...! (*He catches—if possible—the gun*)
Henry Look out! It's *loaded*!
Bill Bloody hell! (*He accidentally fires the gun and hits the cuckoo clock on the* DL *wall. The clock "cuckoos" like mad and the cuckoo itself flies in and out before dropping dead*)

Davenport enters from the kitchen

Davenport What the hell's going on? (*He sees Bill with the gun*) Was it *you* firing that gun?
Bill Certainly was. I think I got a clay pigeon, too. (*He points to the cuckoo clock*)

Vic (*still on his knees*) Can I open my eyes now?

There is a banging on the front door and the doorbell rings urgently. Vic sits on the settee

Slater (*off*) What the hell's going on in there?

Henry unlocks the door

Henry Coming, Sergeant!

Slater enters, still holding the briefcase. He marches DL *and bangs the briefcase down*

Slater Right! Where's that fellow who hit me with his briefcase? (*He sees the Passer-by on the floor*) That's him! What the devil's happened to him?

Henry He fell over.

Slater What was all that shooting about? Who *is* this bloke?

Henry I don't know.

Slater Come on, who is he?!

Henry (*giving in*) OK! I suppose we'd better tell the truth.

Vic What?

Bill **Davenport**	(*together*)	Hang on a second! Wait, Mr Perkins!

Jean **Betty**	(*together*)	Don't do it! There's no need!

Henry No! The game's up. We've had a good run.

Jean **Vic** **Betty** **Davenport** **Bill**	(*together*)	Don't do it! Plead ignorance! Plead ignorance! After all we've been through! You don't have to say anything! Don't chuck it all away, Mr Perkins!

Henry No! I want to confess!

Jean **Vic** **Betty** **Davenport** **Bill**	(*together*)	You don't have to confess! He can't prove anything! Don't say a word! Don't say anything without a lawyer! I'll take care of it, Mr Perkins!

Henry No! It's best for all of us!

Jean			No, it isn't!
Vic			It's not best for me!
Betty	(*together*)		Not another word!
Davenport			You haven't been properly warned!
Bill			I can do my own confessing!

Slater (*interrupting*) Shut up!

They do so immediately

Sit down!

They do immediately, Jean and Betty sitting on the Passer-by

(*To Henry*) You—stand up.

Henry does so

OK. Let's have it.

Henry looks at everybody. He then picks up the "money" briefcase and takes a deep breath

Henry (*to Slater*) I picked up this briefcase by mistake on the Underground. The bloke who took my briefcase ended up in the river in Putney and the bloke who put him in the river in Putney has just ended up with a sprained wrist, a fractured jaw and a broken ankle on my carpet. *That* briefcase, (*he points to Slater's*) as you know, contains some papers, a diary and what is left of a cheese and chutney sandwich. *This* briefcase, (*he holds up his*) contains seven hundred and thirty-five thousand pounds. (*He puts the briefcase down*) Less ten per cent to him. (*He holds out his hand*)

Davenport passes over his bundle of money to Henry

And twenty-five thousand to him. (*He holds out his hand to Vic*)

Vic sadly passes over his bundle of money to Henry

Plus seven thousand five hundred for a car worth five hundred quid.

Vic hands over the second bundle

That wraps up the financial aspect of the matter. (*He hands over the bundles of money to Slater*) Now, on the personal front! She (*he points to Betty*) is not Adelaide the nudist and he (*he points to Vic*) is not Percy the pervert. She is Betty the good friend from Clapham, and he is very plain and very simple Vic. This gentleman (*he points to Davenport*) is not my brother Archie, reliable or otherwise and nor is he a travelling salesman hoping to catch the overnight train to Manchester. He is a p— —(*he hesitates*) part-time drinker in *The Prince of Wales* pub—where I was *not* soliciting and nor do any of us indulge in hanky panky under the blanket. He (*he points to Bill*) has a lot of faults but he is who he says he is. I am *not* Freddy Perkins, this lady's *brother-in-law*. I am Henry Perkins, this lady's *husband*. This briefcase (*he picks up the Passer-by's*) contains the goods, which have caused all the trouble and for which *he* (*he points to Passer-by*) was hoping to receive this, (*he holds up his briefcase*) and when he received *that* (*he points to Slater's briefcase*) he put Mr Nasty in the river and turned up here demanding the return of his brerfcurse.

There is a pause

Slater Say that again.

There is a pause

Henry I picked up this briefcase——
All ⎫ (*together*) ⎧ Never mind!
Slater ⎭ ⎩ Shut up! (*He picks up Passer-by's briefcase, crosses to the telephone table and starts to open it*)
Vic Sergeant, he was going to hand it in from the very beginning.
Henry (*hopelessly*) Vic...!
Betty It was the shock, you see.
Henry (*hopelessly*) Betty...!
Jean He's always been a bit simple-minded.
Henry (*hopelessly*) Jean...!

Slater looks up from the open briefcase

Slater Oy! Coke!

Vic I couldn't drink a thing, honestly.

Slater takes out a couple of polythene bags

Slater No! Cocaine!
All (*amazed*) Cocaine?!

He shows them the contents of the briefcase—several bags of white powder

Slater A whole briefcase full of pure cocaine. You'll get a sizeable reward for this, Mr Perkins.
Henry (*pleased*) Will I?
Slater Yeah. Three thousand pounds at least.
Henry That'll repair the cuckoo clock, anyway. (*He sits in the armchair*)

Slater collects up the briefcase

Slater (*to Henry*) You're a credit to the community, Mr Perkins.
Henry (*nodding*) Yes. (*He sits in the armchair*)
Slater (*to the Passer-by*) Come on, you. (*To Davenport and Bill*) Get him into the ambulance; give me a hand, will you?
Passer-by (*to Vic*) Ik kreck jullie wel Britten! (*Ik kreck yoolie wel Britten! / I will get even with you Britons!*)
Vic Yeah, tell that to the judge!

The Passer-by starts to hop off

Jean You're right, Betty, he does look like an effeminate teapot.

Slater turns, thinking the above remark is referring to him. He glares at them, then exits after Davenport, Bill and the Passer-by

Henry manages a rueful smile

Henry (*cheerfully*) That's it then, Jean! Serve up the roast chicken for the birthday boy.

Jean puts on a cheerful front

Jean Yes. Happy birthday, Henry! (*She sits on the right arm of the armchair*)
Henry Thanks, Jean.

Betty sits on the left arm of the settee

Betty Yes, happy birthday, Henry!
Henry Thanks, Betty.
Vic Happy birthday, Henry!
Henry Thanks, Vic.

Davenport returns through the front door and comes to the left of the armchair

Davenport Just thought I'd say, "no hard feelings", Mr Perkins. (*He holds out his hand*)

Henry takes it

Henry Thanks, Sergeant. I'm sorry you missed out on early retirement, though.

Bill enters from the front door, carrying the suitcase, goes above the armchair to c

Bill Right, come on, let's go!
Vic Go? Where?
Bill London Airport—Barcelona.
Henry Haven't you been listening, Bill? We've lost the lot. Sergeant Slater's gone off with all the cash!
Bill Don't be daft. I switched the money from the briefcase into the suitcase ages ago. (*He opens the suitcase to reveal all the money, which cascades to the floor*)

Curtain music starts

Vic Bloody hell!
Betty Bill!
Henry You're brilliant, Bill, bloody brilliant!

Jean Fantastic!

They all laugh as Bill starts to throw the bundles to them. They, in turn, grab the money and throw it up in the air. Everybody is laughing excitedly and talking at once as——

—the CURTAIN *falls*

FURNITURE AND PROPERTY LIST

Further dressing may be added at the director's discretion

ACT I

On stage: Dining table laid-up for four people in the dining-room
Cupboard. *In it:* **Jean**'s coat, set with both sleeves inside out
Sideboard. *On it:* a selection of liquor bottles and glasses, *Yellow Pages,* a vase of flowers
Long settee
Armchair
Table. *On it:* radio
Small desk. *In it:* passports
Cuckoo clock
Coffee table
Small table. *On it:* phone
Blanket

Off stage: Candle in a silver holder (**Jean**)
Bowl, wooden spoon (**Jean**)
Bowl of peanuts, bottle of sparkling rosé (**Jean**)
Briefcase containing bundles of fifty pound notes wrapped in elastic bands (used throughout) (**Henry**)
Tray with four plates and four sets of cutlery (**Jean**)
Raincoat, small suitcase (**Henry**)
Wrapped present—bottle of wine (**Betty**)
Briefcase containing a pair of wet gloves, wet scarf, papers, small telephone book, cheese and chutney sandwich wrapped in paper napkin (used throughout) (**Slater**)
Henry's suitcase (**Davenport**)

Personal: **Jean:** watch (worn throughout)
Davenport: pass
Bill: slip of paper
Slater: pass
Davenport: bundle of money in raincoat pocket

ACT II

On stage: As before

Off stage: Mug of milk, half full bottle of cooking sherry (**Jean**)
               Steaming teapot (**Slater**)
               Jean's clothes—bra, pants, slip and dress (**Betty**)
               First aid box (**Slater**)
               Briefcase containing bags of white powder (**Passer-by**)
               Henry's suitcase, containing the bundles of money (**Bill**)

Personal: **Vic:** keys
               Passer-by: gun
               Betty: keys

LIGHTING PLOT

Property fittings required: nil
Interior setting. The same throughout

ACT I

To open: Overall general lighting

No cues

ACT II

To open: Overall general lighting

No cues

EFFECTS PLOT

ACT I

Cue 13	**Betty**: "…you lucky devil." *Doorbell rings*	(Page 22)
Cue 14	**Henry**: "…made me christen myself Freddy!" *Phone rings*	(Page 32)
Cue 15	**Henry** goes to open the cupboard *Phone rings*	(Page 34)
Cue 16	**Betty** takes a swig *Phone rings*	(Page 36)
Cue 17	**Henry**: "You'd better get home, for God's sake." *Phone rings*	(Page 37)
Cue 18	**Davenport** moves to **Vic** *Curtain music begins to play*	(Page 53)

ACT II

Cue 19	**Henry**: "…snuff it before the candles." *Phone rings*	(Page 57)
Cue 20	**Jean** is now upright, but with her coat on back to front *Phone rings*	(Page 73)
Cue 21	**Betty**: "Well, be quick, for goodness sake." *Phone rings*	(Page 75)
Cue 22	The **Passer-by** fires the gun *Vase smashes, sending the flowers into the air*	(Page 95)
Cue 23	The **Passer-by** fires the gun *Radio flies off the table* DR *and music is heard—Carmen;* *gradually dies and grinds to a halt*	(Page 96)
Cue 24	**Bill** fires the gun *Cuckoo clock "cuckoos" like mad and the cuckoo itself* *flies in and out before dropping dead*	(Page 96)
Cue 25	There is a banging on the front door *Doorbell rings urgently*	(Page 97)
Cue 26	**Bill** opens the suitcase to reveal all the money *Curtain Music starts*	(Page 101)